DAIDRA SENIOR

KISSES FROM A KILLER

ONE LOVE
PUBLISHING

First published by One Love Publishing 2025

Copyright © 2025 by Daidra Senior

All rights reserved. No part of this publication may be reproduced, stored, or transmitted in any form or by any means, electronic, mechanical, photocopying, recording, scanning, or otherwise without written permission from the publisher. It is illegal to copy this book, post it to a website, or distribute it by any other means without permission.

This novel is entirely a work of fiction. The names, characters, and incidents portrayed in it are the work of the author's imagination. Any resemblance to actual persons, living or dead, events, or localities is entirely coincidental.

Daidra Senior asserts the moral right to be identified as the author of this work.

Designations used by companies to distinguish their products are often claimed as trademarks. All brand names and product names used in this book and on its cover are trade names, service marks, trademarks, and registered trademarks of their respective owners. The publishers and the book are not associated with any product or vendor mentioned in this book. None of the companies referenced within the book have endorsed the book.

First edition

ISBN: 978-1-0697285-1-7

This book was professionally typeset on Reedsy. Find out more at reedsy.com

Dedication
For the ones who survived the silence—
And for those who never got the chance to speak.
To every woman who carries the weight of a buried truth,
and to every girl still learning to trust her voice.
This story is for you.
And to the darkness,
Thank you for teaching me how to write with light.

Contents

	Acknowledgments	iii
1	Scenes of Kisses	1
2	The Taste of Ash and Kisses	9
3	Kisses of Shame	16
4	Bittersweet	33
5	First Kiss	50
6	Silver Foil	56
7	Kisses Too Close	69
8	Wrapped in Guilt	78
9	Beneath the Wrapper	82
10	A kiss Among Thorns	87
11	The Family Kiss	93
12	The Cocoa Code	98
13	Sweet Lies	103
14	Kisses, Take Two	107
15	Sweet Residue	112
16	Tag, Kiss, Run	117
17	Kisses That Turned Bitter	120
18	Kisses That Lied	125
19	Melted Promises	131
20	Kisses Between Cases	134
21	Portrait of a Killer's Kiss	138
22	Burnt Kisses	143
23	The Kiss That Keeps Coming Back	148

24	The Kiss That Connects Them	153
25	No Questions, Just Kisses	156
26	Kisses He Tried to Take Back	160
27	Kisses of the Past	165
28	Kisses from the Wrong Woman	170
29	Kisses of Glitter and Ghosts	178
30	Kisses from Honeycomb	185
31	Kisses Between the Lines	190
32	Bittersweet Trails	196
33	Bitters on the Tongue	201
34	The Honeycomb Pact	206
35	Kisses in Code	215
36	Foil and Fragments	220
37	Shards of Sweetness	226
38	Dark Chocolate	231
39	Melted Truths	234
40	The Origin of the Kiss	243
41	The Wrappers She Kept	250
42	Echoes of Kisses	254
43	The Name Behind the Kiss	261
44	Final Kiss	268
45	Aftertaste	274
Also by Daidra Senior		281

Acknowledgments

Writing *Kisses From a Killer* was a journey through shadows, both of the mind and of the world we live in. This book would not exist without the support, patience, and inspiration of several people who kept me grounded while letting me explore the darkest corners of human nature.

First, I must thank my family and friends for believing in me, even when the story got unsettling and the nights grew long. Your encouragement, quiet confidence, and occasional nudges reminded me that stories, no matter how dark, need to be told.

To my editors, beta readers, and early reviewers, your insights sharpened the suspense, kept the twists plausible, and reminded me that tension works best when grounded in truth. Your patience and honesty were invaluable.

To the readers who pick up this book looking for a thrill, a mystery, or a twist, you are the ultimate reason any story matters. Thank you for leaping into this world I've created.

1

Scenes of Kisses

A Rastafarian was found in his fourth-floor Iris Street apartment in a pool of blood. Yet there were no cuts, no struggle, no wounds to explain it. He'd been dead for nearly a day before anyone noticed. His wrists were bound with duct tape, the skin beneath it bruised and swollen. Charles Libra, six feet three, broad-shouldered, looked as if he had surrendered.

The beige curtains fluttered in the cold air drifting through the half-open window. A once red and white carpet now cradled Charles Libra's body. His eyes were wide, frozen in a final stare. Beside him, a coffee table stood undisturbed, a bouquet rising from its vase. Other than the corpse, the room was untouched, almost pristine.

The sharp scent of pine drifted through the apartment. A television blaring next door pierced the silence.

Detective Myrna Watkis woke to the shrill ring of her flip phone. Her strawberry-blond hair tangled across her face as she rolled out of bed, clutching her throbbing head. She'd celebrated her promotion the night before, and the consequences lingered behind her eyes.

The voice on the other end was her sergeant

"Hello," she croaked.

"Morning, Detective. Hope I didn't wake you."

"No, sergeant. I wasn't sleeping."

"Good. You dressed?"

"I can be dressed in five."

"Don't bother changing. I want you sharp, not polished. We've got one, a body, male, found in a locked apartment on Iris Street, and something's off."

Her breath came out shaky, the kind that felt too light to control, and she pressed a hand briefly to her abdomen.

"You want me to ride backup?"

"No, I want you to take it, your case."

A tiny smile tugged at her lips before she could stop it, but the sudden chill running up her arms forced her to swallow hard.

"My case?"

"You passed the boards. You wear the badge now. I'll be nearby if you screw it up...don't screw it up! Pack smart, we may be chasing shadows for a while."

"Understood. I'll be there in twenty."

"Make it fifteen. And Watkis?"

"Yeah."

"Don't try to solve it all at once. Let the scene talk to you, and listen."

He hung up. Myrna stood for a moment in the dead silence of her bedroom, then peeled herself out of the clothes she'd passed out in. In the kitchen, she poured black coffee into a travel mug and grabbed her coat, keys, and notebook. Just like that, her first real case was waiting.

Myrna's apartment was immaculate, a white living room with satin sheets and everything in its place; a sharp contrast to the chaos she was driving into. Upon opening the front door, Myrna was met with a brisk spring draft. It was the time of year that lent itself to a lot of rain and cool breeze. The snow was slowly washing away. Myrna looked around and noticed the slush of the Canadian weather. She closed her jacket, stepped out onto the barren street and quickly got into her gray Honda. It was roughly a twenty-minute drive from her Kanata home to Iris Street. Using her flashing lights, Myrna made it in ten. The neighbourhood was a cluster of low-income housing, known locally as 'the projects.' Crowds of onlookers pressed against yellow police tape, flapping in the wind. Myrna parked and spotted Sergeant Moses striding toward her. Myrna slowly sipped her coffee.

"You made good time," he said without looking up.

"Didn't want to be late for my first corpse."

"Cute. Keep that humour, it'll help. Just don't crack wise in front of the press or family." He gestured toward the building. "We've got a time of death. M.E. put it late last night."

"Any witnesses?"

"A night janitor saw a green car pull out around 1 a.m. No plates, no make. That's what you're working with."

Myrna nodded,

"understood."

"Build your timeline and keep your notes tight. If you get stuck, I'm a call away. But this isn't training wheels anymore."

"Got it."

He stepped closer, lowering his voice.

"First cases are like first lovers, you never forget them, and sometimes they don't forget you either." He walked off, leaving Myrna in the hush of the crime scene. Inside, Myrna flashed her badge. Several men exchanged looks as she walked in, their smirks and raised brows greeting her before any words did. Circling the living room, she crossed her arms, lips pulled tight in her habit of thought.

The window was half open, the zephyr slipping through the curtains like a whisper.

"Is this how the window was found?" she asked a uniform.

"It was wide open, along with the other. Got chilly, so we pulled it down a bit."

Myrna's eyes narrowed. She stepped into the young officer's space.

"Are you kidding me? Where'd you get your badge, at a flea market? You'd better not have compromised my crime scene."

The officer shrank back. Myrna turned to the room once again. The small dining table held a vase of flowers and two plastic cups. Something about the room made her skin prickle, as if the violence had been wiped clean. It didn't make sense. A man that big, subdued as if his strength had crumpled like paper.

The stillness of the room pressed like a held breath, heavier than any fight could have left behind. Libra's once-rich skin had drained to an eerie olive, and the open window gave no hint of forced entry. The blood pooled beneath him, thick and startling, yet no lacerations marked his body.

Then Myrna noticed the dreadlocks. Cut clean, spread across the carpet like discarded rope. The dread was covered in bacon grease. Myrna crouched near the body, thoughts spinning, when a small, straight-faced female walked into the room.

"You must be Myrna, I'm your new partner, Dessa Simms," she said, smiling with her hand extended.

"Some crazy scene, huh?" Her voice thinned into a whisper; her eyes never stopped wandering, wide and curious. Myrna rose, shaking it graciously. She noticed her partner's subtle beauty, striking against the grim scene.

"Yah, it's a real mess, indeed. We got our work cut out for us." Myrna replied, smoothing a nonexistent wrinkle from her sleeve.

Dessa moved slowly around the room, eyes sharp. Near a wooden table, she stooped and picked something up.

"Don't touch that!" Myrna snapped

"You're not wearing any gloves."

"Oh shoot, I'm such a bubble head sometimes."

"I have them right here in my pocket." Placing the razor in a bag that Myrna had. Dessa twisted her black, relaxed hair into a bun and made her way around the room while putting on the gloves.

Libra's wrists formed an X across his chest. His mouth was gagged with what seemed like a ripped t-shirt. His cleaner had been the one to find him. Myrna took her aside to ask her some questions. Trembling, the middle-aged woman gently brushed back her straggly grey hair.

"It's a disgrace," the house cleaner said, lowering her quivering hands,

"To dishonour the man like that."

"What do you mean?" asked Myrna as she gently reached out and touched her shoulder. She began shaking her head from side to side.

"Mr. Libra was a true Rastafarian; he never ate meat or any meat product, so to see him covered..." Her shoulders hitched, and the tissue couldn't keep up with the wetness gathering beneath her eyes. She wiped her tears, and Myrna had an officer escort her outside for some fresh air.

Dessa stooped over the body. Using a pen, she bridged a gap between the t-shirt gag and Libra's teeth.

"Hey, there's something in his mouth!"

Myrna bent closer.

"What is it?"

Carefully, Dessa shifted the pen beneath the gag.

"I'm not sure, it looks like raw meat."

Myrna recoiled, face twisting until her glasses nearly shook off.

"That's disgusting. How did I miss that?"

"I eat a lot of carrots," Dessa quipped.

"What did the witness have to say?"

"Not much," Myrna admitted.

"She usually cleans on Wednesdays. Said Libra was a strict vegetarian. She found him like this and called us."

Dessa's eyes swept the room again.

"Wow. Ironic. Does anyone else live here?" Myrna motioned toward the family picture on the yellow wall beside them.

"He had two kids and a common-law wife, but they're out of town."

"Then why cover him in grease?" Dessa murmured.

The two detectives stood there for a moment, staring at the slickened dreadlocks, each waiting for the other to offer an explanation that wouldn't come.

Dessa fell silent, her gaze lingering on the family photo, a faint crease between her brows.

Both women made their way into the other rooms of the apartment. The bathroom was clean, and a glass vase sat on the toilet tank, dried petals embedded in a bed of shiny stones. Nothing unusual was found except a bag of weed inside the toilet tank. The children's rooms were typical, featuring pictures of happy children and toys.

The couple's bedroom was decorated in red and black. The bed had not been made, and a condom wrapper was found lying on the floor. No sign of a condom used or otherwise. The elderly neighbour, Mr. Jacob, hard of hearing with his TV blaring, hadn't noticed a thing.

Four weeks later, Myrna received a call from Dr. Festus, a sexist coroner she hated dealing with. The results of Charles' autopsy were ready. Myrna called Dessa immediately. They were to meet up there at the coroner's office. On arriving, Dessa paused at the doorway, smoothing her palm over her stomach as her breath hitched. Her steps slowed as the chemical-clean scent hit her. Too sharp and too cold; she kept her eyes off the metal doors lining the walls. Myrna waved her over and warned her about Dr. Festus's sexist attitude.

"Hello girls, mind if I join your twosome?"

"I don't float that way," Dessa answered. Myrna rolled her eyes, her expression flat as pavement.

"Look, can we get down to business?"

"Time of death between 9 and 10 p.m., the night before he was found, Tuesday, April 5th," Festus said briskly.

"Toxicology shows antihistamines, which explain the lack of struggle. And what you found in his mouth—" he hesitated,

"—was a piece of a male member." Dessa's eyes widened. Myrna's heart skipped a beat, and she felt her stomach twist.

"They cut off his penis and put it in his mouth?" She blurted.

"Not exactly." Dr. Festus pulled back the sheet to reveal Charles's penis, fully intact, wearing a condom.

"There was no intercourse. The blood he laid in wasn't his, either."

Dessa stepped forward

"What, then, whose blood was it?"

"That I don't know as yet, not all the results are in, still testing. What I can tell you is this: he was strangled. Flat on his back. The killer straddled him."

Myrna blinked hard, her brows knitting as she stared at the intact penis and the empty blood tray, like the pieces no longer fit the board. The pool of blood nagged at her. Strangulation didn't bleed. Something was off, horribly off. And the obvious question, whose penis was it? Myrna's grip tightened on her pen, her stomach sinking as the implications snapped together in her mind, one chilling click at a time. Everything now hinted at the chilling thought that another body was out there somewhere waiting to be discovered.

2

The Taste of Ash and Kisses

The scent of scorched flesh clung to the cold air, thick with smoke and secrets burned to ash. A janitor had found the body just after noon, bound, burned and stuffed into a storage closet no one had touched in weeks. A single gunshot had obliterated Johnson's mouth. A bag of chocolate kisses rested in his pocket, untouched by the flames. A security guard jacket hung on a hook that looked down at the corpse, which was collapsed on its knees. The closet door had been latched from the outside. The badge on the jacket read Harry Johnson.

"You smell that?" Dessa whispered, squinting through the dim hallway.

"Like week-old rotten eggs and sulphur," Myrna wrinkled her nose.

"Embalming fluid," she said quietly.

"He was preserved. The burns were inflicted long after he died."

The hallway reeked of death and burned flesh and secrets long buried. She swallowed hard, the taste of ash catching in her throat like a warning that wouldn't go down. She pulled on gloves. They crouched by the open closet. The heat had eaten through Johnson's torso, skin charred black from the waist up. Myrna shifted the light downward and froze.

"Dessa... look."

The lower half of the body was intact enough to show what was missing, completely missing. Dessa's breath caught. She didn't need to say the word; she had seen it every day for the last three weeks, floating in a sterile specimen jar at the morgue, a 'John Doe' trophy with no owner, until now.

"Jesus... that's..."

"The missing piece from the Libra case," Myrna whispered, the beam of her flashlight trembling slightly.

The silence in the closet grew heavy. The math was simple but sickening. If they'd had the piece for weeks, and Harry was only found today, he had been a "supply closet" for the killer long before Charles Libra ever crossed their radar.

The body was easily concealed on the far wing of the building, which had been under construction for some time. There were many warning signs for civilians. Do not enter; danger and that sort of thing. Cement bags were stacked in a corner near a staircase. There were ashes from burnt clothing on the cement floor, and no footprint could be seen. A thin veil of soot clung to the low ceiling of the storage closet, turning the cramped space into a darkened chamber. The scorch marks on the wall started only at waist height, sharp, irregular streaks that fanned upward like fingers dragging through smoke. The concrete below was untouched, cold, clean, as though the fire had been carefully contained to his upper body. Nothing in the room showed panic. No overturned shelves, no signs of struggle and no desperate scrapes on the floor. And that was the part Myrna found most disturbing. Whoever killed Harry Johnson had taken their time.

By the next morning, the second body had already rewritten the rules of the case. The blinds were half-drawn. Sunlight filtered in slats across the floor, falling just short of the polished shoes of Sergeant Moses, a tall man with shoulders like a fence post and a voice designed to flatten egos. Myrna stood stiffly near the window, hands clasped behind her back.

Dessa sat perched on the edge of a cracked leather chair, thumb running along her coffee cup, as though it might split open under pressure. The Sergeant didn't look up from the report he was flipping through.

"You want to tell me what the hell's going on with this case?"

Myrna swallowed, palms sweaty.

"We're still assembling...."

He cut her off,

"That's not what I asked. I don't need a thesis, Watkis. I need answers. Two men are dead. One with his junk stuffed in the other's mouth like some goddamn horror show. The press is circling, the mayor's calling me at home, and you're telling me you're still 'assembling'?"

Dessa pushed herself up slowly, as if testing the moment.

"Sir, we're working the connections. The victims didn't know each other personally, but we believe there's a shared link, possibly a woman."

Sergeant Moses stood up, placing both palms on his desk. His voice cracked through the room like a whip.

"Possibly? That's the best you got?"

Myrna thought to herself, maybe they're right; perhaps I am in over my head. Then she thought, No, I can solve this. She straightened up and continued.

"Sir, the body was preserved. You can smell it, embalming fluid. That means Johnson's been dead for weeks." That changes our timeline."

The Sergeant finally looked up, his sharp brown eyes narrowing.

"So you're saying he was a cold case, re-heated? Myrna shrugged,

"Something like that, sir." Moses reacted coldly.

"You have zero suspects. You have zero motive. And you've got my phones lighting up like Christmas." He slapped the folder shut.

"Tell me, Watkis. Did I make a mistake putting you on this case?" Myrna didn't flinch.

"No, sir. You didn't."

"Then prove it. You've got one week. After that, I start pulling strings, and one of them might be yours. Dismissed."

As the door slammed behind them, Dessa said low enough that only the air heard her,

"I liked him better when he was yelling about parking spaces." Myrna just exhaled slowly, eyes fixed ahead.

"We need something, and fast."

"I agree,"

"Meet me at my place, I'm going to grab some Chinese food, and we're going to pull an all-nighter," Dessa unlocked her red Toyota Tercel. Myrna agreed, and the two women separated to meet later at Dessa's four-storey apartment building.

Dessa lived on the second floor in a modest two-bedroom apartment with a small balcony. The apartment had been furnished with furniture bought from IKEA. The second bedroom was decorated in pink, as it was her mother's favourite colour. Dessa had made a point of cleaning off the bed, which is usually loaded with clothing. She knew that Myrna would probably have to stay over. The idea was to go through the two cases with a fine-tooth comb until they came up with something concrete.

Around 7 p.m., Myrna buzzed Dessa's apartment. She let her in, and Myrna noticed immediately that Dessa was not the cleaning fanatic that she was. After they had finished eating dinner, the two began working. Myrna was now slowly getting to like Dessa, despite her cleaning habits. She liked the fact that Dessa was a hard worker. She'd finally found a partner who was as driven as she was.

"Let's start with where they went to school," Dessa said.

"Harry is from America, and Charles was schooled here in Ottawa," answered Myrna.

"What about the history of employment?" Dessa asked, determined.

"Well, Myrna began, before he was a disc jockey, Charles worked as a security guard."

"Yes, and so was Harry."

"Now we have a connection," both ladies said at once.

"Could be a coworker," Dessa said, narrowing her eyes. "Someone with a grudge."

"Or a lover," Myrna countered.

"We'll run both angles tomorrow." She glanced at the wall clock. "Quarter past one."

"Go ahead," Dessa said.

"I'll keep at it."

Myrna stretched her fingers once, twice, like they'd been gripping something invisible for hours. Her eyelids fluttered in slow blinks, each one longer than the last.

"Try not to drown in coffee," she hinted as she disappeared

into the spare room. Alone, Dessa turned back to the evidence board. Charles: strangled, plastered with bacon grease, his locks sheared. Harry: bound, shot, burned. Different methods, same message. She scrawled one word in red across the center: **DISGRACE**.

As the red ink of **DISGRACE** dried on the board, Dessa leaned back, her mind drifting to how different her life had been just a month ago, before the pressure of the Sergeant and the grim reality of the Libra case had taken over.

She remembered that at the end of her first shift with Myrna, she'd gone straight to a West Indian restaurant on King Edward Ave. She ordered her favourite, oxtail and rice and peas with vegetables and a tall glass of carrot juice. Since she lived alone, for now, Dessa hardly ever cooked, and cleaning was no exception.

She was a straight female who functioned like a typical male. Tidiness was never her strength, which became a sore point between her and her sister, Deshauna. That particular evening, her clothes lay on the floor, and the sink was filled with dishes. Dessa had pledged to wash the dishes and pick up the clothes just as soon as she'd finished eating. As usual, she fell asleep on the sofa in front of the television.

Dessa wasn't as seasoned in police work as Myrna, but she had been a detective for two years. She spent most of her career in Toronto. She chose to relocate to Ottawa to get her mother closer to her siblings. Caring for her had taken its toll, and she decided, along with her family members, that she could use the support. Dessa was more than capable of hiring proper care for her mom, but felt obligated to care for her herself. Her mother had always been there for her, so that's why she couldn't pass her off to strangers.

Mother had a mild case of dementia and needed to be watched every hour of the day. Dessa's brother and two sisters were all living in Ottawa. They had been encouraging her for years to move from Toronto. Finally, she had decided to give in to her family. The week before the move, her mother had fallen and broken her hip. This made it difficult for her to travel. As Dessa had to report to work, one of her siblings went down to stay with her mom until she was able to make the move.

3

Kisses of Shame

Earlier, the morning after Charles Libra's body was found, Myrna shuffled into the kitchen, eyes half-closed, and wrapped both hands around her coffee mug like she needed its warmth to stay standing. Her head still hummed from the night before, the echoes of champagne and too much laughter lingering in her bones.

Myrna was part of a tight circle of friends who had known each other since grade school. Mona, the most outgoing, had arrived the night before with champagne in hand, wearing a tight red spandex dress that left little to the imagination. Her long, curly black hair spilled across her shoulders as she raised the bottle high.

"Let's party, girl," she'd shouted, dragging Myrna into a night that was loud, wild, and full of promise. Now, the apartment was silent except for the whisper of the curtains as they swayed in the breeze drifting through the open window. Myrna pressed her palms against her eyes. The glitter of last night already felt like it belonged to someone else. Her thoughts drifted, uninvited, to her parents, both lawyers who had raised her to believe success meant Harvard or Yale. Myrna had grown used to the looks she got; the kind that said she should've been anything *but* a cop. She remembered the day her parents sat her down to ask which university she would attend, Harvard or Yale, their alma mater.

"I'm not going to university," she said, forcing a smile that wabbled at the edges even as her chin lifted a notch too high.

Her father's eyes widened, face reddening.

"That's ridiculous, Myrna. You don't know what you're saying. Of course, you want to go to university; it's all we've talked about."

"Father, with all due respect, you're the one who's always said that."

Her mother stepped in gently.

"Peter, why not hear her out? Forcing her won't help. She won't perform."

It took weeks, but eventually her father relented. At five-foot-seven and one hundred and thirty pounds, Myrna walked into the police training camp and found herself surrounded by a sea of men. Ten women started; only five remained by the end. She closed her eyes, letting the memories fade, and placed the case files on Dessa's side table, and slowly drifted off to sleep.

Dessa continued to work. Harry Johnson's body was found in a begging position, arms lifted, head tilted skyward, knees pressed to the floor, suggesting that he, too, had been humiliated. Both men knew their killer because he or she was able to get so close. Charles's size and the absence of any struggle suggested familiarity. Both men are Black, and more than likely, so is the killer. Dessa noted, cautiously. Sometimes, killers stay within their own racial group.

Finally, she climbed into bed. Pushing aside the clothes on her bed, she wasted no time in falling asleep. The next morning, she awoke early to find Myrna in the kitchen making breakfast. She'd made her famous cheese and pepper omelet, which Dessa enjoyed thoroughly.

"You're just in time," she said, adjusting the long blond braid she often wore.

"Boy, I thought I was up early, but you got me beat."

"I had a look at your evidence board, it looks good."

"Thanks." The two ladies ate quickly, barely pausing between bites, their chairs scraping back the moment they mentioned the office building on Merivale Road, where both Charles and Harry had once worked.

Myrna fought her way up through Orleans, Nepean, and eventually into cold cases, always proving, always pushing. Nepean was where she'd learned the most, riding alongside Bob Regnard, a seasoned officer who became more mentor than partner, teaching her the rhythms of real detective work. After four years on cold cases, she applied downtown, scored the highest on the detective exam, and beat out two male officers. The reaction had been mixed: the women cheered her, most of the men stayed quiet, and Bob, of course, was the first to shake her hand.

At the Merivale office, they came face to face with a bushy-haired desk clerk. He was skinny with a high-pitched voice. He directed them to the 8th floor to Mr. Stowe. John was the one in charge of personnel.

"Mr. Stowe, Detective Myrna Watkis," she said, showing her badge.

"This is my partner, Dessa Simms. We're investigating the

murders of Charles Libra and Harry Johnson. We think they were both employed here."

"How can I be of help?" Stowe asked.

"They both worked as security guards for your company," answered Dessa.

"We would like to speak with the other employees that they worked with," began Myrna.

"Can you direct us to where we may do that?"

"There is a monthly meeting held here at 3 p.m. today. Otherwise, it would be quite difficult to find them all in one place."

"Thank you very much, we'll be back at 3 p.m." Dessa smiled, and the two officers left the building. They had barely cleared the curb when the radio cracked again. 'Possible fatal at Rockcliffe Lookout,' dispatch said. 'Update...vehicle rollover. Evidence suggests it may be connected. Myrna's head veered toward the speaker. Dessa's fingers tightened on the steering wheel. When they arrived on scene, the night air still carried the sharp metallic scent of twisted metal and lake water. An officer held up a plastic evidence bag. Inside, stuck to a jagged scrap of paper were clumped strands of dreadlocks, dark, matted, unmistakably real; twisted to form the words *'Burn in hell.'*

A few feet away, tire grooves carved deep scars through the gravel shoulder. The van's headlights pointed crookedly toward the water below, one flickering weakly. Spray residue, orange and oily, streaked the driver's side window.

"The pepper spray hit him before he lost control," a constable said, shining his light over the shattered glass. Down by the rocks, paramedics stood in a tight circle around a body lying unnaturally twisted, as though tossed there by an unseen hand. His shirt was soaked through, the water around him stained a faint rust. Myrna stepped closer to the body bag as the paramedics hovered, waiting for the okay to lift. Vogney's limbs were twisted at sharp angles, his shirt clinging wetly to his ribs. Only a small bruise darkened his temple, a mark that could pass for blunt impact, but was just as common in a rollover. Dessa angled her flashlight, watching the beam glide across his face, his chest, the bent wrist.

"Impact threw him clean out of the van," she uttered.

"Looks that way," Myrna replied.

Uphill, the van creaked in the wind, metal shifting like an injured animal trying to breathe. The headlights continued their weak, desperate flicker. Inside, the orange haze of pepper spray hung in the air, stinging even from a distance. One of the uniformed officers coughed and lifted his sleeve.

"Whoever hit him with that knew what they were doing. He didn't stand a chance behind the wheel."

Myrna didn't answer; her eyes moved from the smashed windshield to the carved-up gravel where the tires had torn through the shoulder. A straight shot, no sign of braking, no sign of struggle besides the chaos the crash left behind.

Behind her, the paramedics began to zip the bag, the rasp of the zipper cutting through the afternoon air.

Dessa wiped the spray from her eyes.

"What do you think?"

Myrna shook her head once.

"I think Festus will tell us what the body says."

She stepped back, giving the team room to lift the stretcher. The air felt heavier now, thick with lake spray and the cold edge of something calculated. Dessa exhaled slowly, and a spark of heat flickered behind her stare.

"The killer struck again!"

"I don't understand this killer. Why connect the dots for us?" Myrna's voice frayed at the edges.

"Maybe he or she feels clever. I mean, other than the obvious placements at the crime scenes, what do we know?" answered Dessa.

Vogney's van sat half-buried in the ditch, metal peeled back like wet cardboard. Dozens of juice bottles, his delivery stock, were jammed between the crushed seats. A few split open and dripped sticky trails down the floor mats. Loose papers clung to the damp gravel, and glossy prints of women in tight dresses and beach poses fluttered in the wind, some plastered against the warped frame of the van.

Dessa crouched, lifting one of the photos between two fingers.

"Man had a type."

Myrna leaned into the cruiser and tapped the keys on the onboard terminal.

"Let's see if he links to Johnson or Libra."

The mobile unit chirped as it processed the query. Screen after screen scrolled past delivery routes, shift logs, and a write-up for chronic lateness. There were no security guard licenses, no shared employers and no overlapping contracts shown.

Dessa angled the monitor toward her.

"Nothing. Not even temp work."

Myrna exhaled slowly, eyes drifting back to the wreck, the jammed juice bottles, the twisted metal, the glossy photos of women scattered like confetti from a party gone wrong.

"So he didn't run in their circles," she muttered, blinking slowly as if asking for patience.

"Not even close."

The air felt heavier. The distance between the victims was widening, not tightening.

The interviews at the security office on Merivale Road went nowhere fast. Employees came in one at a time, settling into the metal chair across from Myrna and Dessa, their uniforms creasing loudly in the quiet room.

"Harry?" one guard said with a faint smile.

"Man was a clown. Always cracking some foolishness. Made the long shifts feel shorter."

Another nodded.

"Yeah, he brightened up the place. Everybody liked him."

But when Charles Libra's name came up, the energy shifted. Shoulders sank, eyes slid to the floor.

"He barely talked," a supervisor admitted.

"Came in, signed his sheet, did his patrol. Never mixed."

A young guard added,

"He wasn't rude or anything, just kept outta people's way."

They asked about Tuesday, April 5th. Alibis stacked up quickly: shift logs, timestamped entries, phone screenshots. Most people were either on-site or at home with their family. Only one guard faltered: a tiny woman with a uniform two sizes too big. She swung her legs under the chair, her feet nowhere near touching the floor.

"Where were you Tuesday night?" Dessa asked.

"Home with my dog," she said, hands clasped in her lap.

Dessa's brow arched slightly, the same thought crossing both their minds.

Not her, not because she couldn't drag a body, but because nothing about her size or presence suggested she could restrain a grown man, strangle him, burn him, poison him, or rig a van without anyone noticing.

When asked who Charles had been close to, only one name surfaced.

"Santana Osborne," said a supervisor.

"She came by a few times. The only one I ever see him chat with."

Myrna jotted the name down.

By the time the last guard left, the room felt heavy, too many dead ends, not enough clarity. Dessa flipped the interview sheet closed with a sigh. Myrna flipped through the personnel files one more time as the last guard stepped out. Harry Johnson was forty; he'd been married twice, with an ex-wife living in Scarborough and a current wife listed at a Nepean address. No kids and no dependents. His file was strangely bare for a man his age, no disciplinary notes, no commendations, nothing that said who he really was.

Rumours, however, filled the gaps. A few guards had danced around it, choosing their words carefully, but the meaning was clear enough. Harry had a wandering eye, and more than one person believed he'd stepped out on his wife more than once.

None of it explained why he'd been found kneeling, humiliated, or why a piece of him had been shoved into Charles Libra's mouth. Two men with nothing obvious in common, no shared address, no shared family, no shared record.

But Myrna couldn't shake the feeling settling in the back of her mind. This felt personal, and personal usually meant a woman was somewhere in the middle.

Myrna's phone buzzed on the table.

She glanced at the screen.

Festus: *Harry's autopsy is ready.*

Myrna stood immediately.

"Let's go."

They entered a clinical basement-level facility attached to the city morgue, tucked behind the General Hospital on Smyth Road. The entrance was discreet, marked only by a frosted glass door with faded black lettering: 'Forensic Services, Authorized Personnel Only.' Inside, the air was perpetually cold and carried the sharp scent of antiseptic mixed with something metallic, faintly reminiscent of old blood.

"Okay, ladies... looking hot today."

Festus said it with a grin that died the moment Dessa's eyes snapped toward him.

"Dude, please," she fired back, dripping sarcasm.

Colour surged up Festus's neck, blooming across his cheeks like a rash.

Myrna tried and failed to hide her chuckle.

"Well," said Festus, clearing his throat.

"This man was overkilled."

Myrna frowned.

"Define overkilled."

"He was drained of blood, injected with embalming fluid, then shot in the mouth and finally set on fire."

Dessa blinked quickly.

"All that after he was already dead?"

Festus nodded.

"Organ failure from blood loss was enough. The rest was theatre."

"What about the time of death?"

"He's been dead about six weeks, which puts the time of death around the third week in February."

Myrna walked toward Dr. Festus's calendar.

"Six weeks would be around February 22...Tuesday. Oh shit!"

"How has this guy been dead for over a month and no one missed him?"

"Your job to figure that out, toots." Myrna shifted her weight forward, just enough for Festus to straighten up.

"Let's go, Simms, we've got some work to do,"

With that, the two ladies left to go back to their division. Now the evidence board had three victims: Vogney—Black male, five-foot-eight, one hundred and eighty-five pounds; Libra—Black male, six-foot-three, two hundred and ten pounds; and Johnson—Black male, five-foot-ten, one hundred and ninety-five pounds. Every scene tried to sell a story that wasn't true. The way they were staged, the bodies seemed to shout one cause of death until Festus peeled back the lie.

Myrna had been left alone for a week. Dessa went out of town to visit her mother, who had taken ill suddenly. During the week alone, she had spent a considerable amount of time reviewing the board and interviews until she was exhausted.

"It felt deliberate," Myrna murmured, holding the tiny foil wrapper between gloved fingers.

"Like the killer wanted us to feel something, not romance, something else entirely. These aren't love tokens. They're kisses of shame. But why only at one crime scene?"

Unfortunately, she was no closer to solving the case. She welcomed Dessa's return to get the help she needed. That same old problem surfaced again, all the men in the force looking at her, watching to see when she would fail. This job was such a boys' club.

This afternoon, she was on her way to interview Santana Osbourne. Santana was standing beside a used Honda, pretending to read the spec sheet, when she spotted Myrna crossing the lot.

Her shoulders twitched just enough to betray the truth: she didn't have anything left to give.

"Detective," she said, breath shaky.

"I'm... uh... I'm at work, so if this is quick, fine. If it's not, come back later."

Her voice was brittle, not hostile, just exhausted. Myrna softened her tone.

"I'm sorry to come here. I won't take much of your time."

Santana nodded once, arms crossing tightly as if she were physically holding herself together.

"What do you want to ask?"

"It's about Sue."

Santana's breath left her in a single, sharp exhale, almost a sob.

"Of course it is," she whispered. "Of course."

She looked away, blinking hard at the sunlight reflecting off the car's hood. When she finally spoke, her voice trembled.

"Yeah, okay. Fine. I know they were screwing around."

Her throat caught.

"I asked Charles about it. He denied it. Lied right to my face."

Her fingers tapped against her bicep, fast and uneven.

"And then he'd swear they were just friends... like I'm stupid. Like I can't see."

She swallowed, blinking fast, staring anywhere but at the detective. Myrna exchanged a worried glance.

"Santana," she said softly, "you don't have to..."

"I *do* have to," Santana cut in, voice cracking.

"Because he's gone. And now I'm stuck here trying to sell cars like my life isn't..."

"Santana!"

A voice boomed from across the lot. Her boss, a stocky man

with a sales badge bouncing on his belt, waved her over.

"Client on the line. Now!"

Santana shut down instantly, breath held, shoulders squared. Mask back on.

"Detective, I can't, I gotta go."

"Santana, we can reschedule..." Myrna started.

She shook her head, eyes shiny.

"No. Not now. Not here."

Her boss shouted again, louder this time.

"Santana! Let's go!"

Santana stepped back, already turning away.

"If you need more... come find me later. Just not today."

She hurried off before Myrna could respond, wiping at her eye once with the back of her hand, quick and angry, the kind of gesture someone hopes no one notices.

Myrna watched her go, knowing she'd barely scratched the surface. She left the used car lot with Santana's last words still nagging at her and drove straight back to the precinct. The lot was nearly full when she pulled in, but one car stood out, Dessa's, dusted with winter salt.

Dessa was already inside, warming her hands around a coffee mug, when Myrna walked through the doors.

"You're back," Myrna said.

"Got in an hour ago, mom's doing better, so I figured I'd jump right in. You look like you've had a day."

"Try a week," she rubbed at her temple as she said it. Her phone buzzed before she could say more. She glanced at the screen.

"Festus! Vogney's results are ready. He wants us at the coroner's office."

Dessa set her coffee aside and stood.

"Alright. Let's go see what he's found."

Within moments, they were back outside, heading to Myrna's car and pulling out of the precinct lot toward the coroner's building. Vogney, who they originally thought died from blunt force trauma caused by the accident, turned out to have died from a heart attack.

"Vogney," Dr. Festus began, "was suffering from coronary artery disease, so his heart was weak. Stress alone could have triggered failure."

"How does that spell murder?"

Myrna crouched beside the victim, squinting at the mottled red marks across his face.

"Burns?" she asked.

The coroner nodded.

"Looks chemical, most likely pepper spray."

"How would someone spray him while driving without being in the vehicle?" Dessa wondered, voice low. No one had an answer.

Inside the forensics lab, low white noise buzzed; centrifuges spun, computers hummed, and fluorescent lights cast a sterile glow over everything. A stout, long-haired brunette stood at a counter with protective eyewear intact. She raised her head to see Simms and Watkis approaching.

"Oh, I'm glad you're here,"

"I just finished the findings on Charles Libra."

"I found no usable fingerprints except one on the razor. That would be yours, officer," she said, looking at Simms.

"Yeah, she picked it up without gloves at the crime scene," Myrna answered.

"What else have you found?"

"The blood is confirmed to be Harry Johnson's blood. The

body was not moved; he was killed in the home."

"What was used to strangle him?" Myrna asked.

"He was strangled with this." She held up a torn cotton t-shirt, stretched and twisted to about 18 inches in length.

"The killer could have been male or female, weighing 120 pounds or more, given the sedative used."

"The razor was used to cut off his locks."

"Wow, this dude is a real nut job," Dessa suggested.

"What makes you think it's a dude?"

"I don't know, maybe it is a woman," she answered. Myrna turned to look back at the C.S.I. agent.

"Did you find any fingerprints on Vogney's vehicle?"

"We haven't finished processing Vogney's crime scene as yet." Dessa's phone rang. She answered. It was one of the techs analyzing the computers.

"We have to go,"

"What's up?" Myrna inquired.

"They found something on the computers."

"And one more thing," the C.S.I. added, flipping through the last page of her report.

"We pulled this from the kitchen sink: burned plastic, porcelain fragments, synthetic hair... dolls melted and tossed like trash."

"Doll parts?" Dessa raised her brows. The agent nodded.

"Looked ritualistic."

Myrna's stomach turned. A child's toy, meant to comfort, was dismembered and discarded like evidence of a forgotten innocence.

"Jesus," the word escaped her as she stepped back.

"That's not just twisted, that's... symbolic." Myrna turned to Dessa.

"We've got a killer who doesn't just want to punish; they want us to see them, understand them, feel it." Dessa's jaw clenched.

"And whoever they are, they're not done talking."

The two said goodbye and headed back to headquarters on the second floor, where the technical crew was located.

"Hey Mark," said Myrna,

"What you got for me?"

"Well," said Mark, all three men like to visit porn sites regularly. One site in particular, 'brown suga.com,'

"Freaks," Dessa said with scorn. Myrna looked at her and smiled, knowing she was thinking the same thing.

"Anything else?" Dessa inquired.

"Two people came up on Johnson and Libra's computers, Pamela Darah and Jacob Asher. There was a picture of Darah on Libra's computer and e-mails mentioning her on Johnson's."

"O.K., thanks, we'll check it out," Myrna stepped past him, already shifting into motion.

"What about the surveillance camera from the sports complex?" she continued,

"There's no image of anyone entering at or close to the time of the murder. The regular comings and goings ended at 8 p.m. when the complex closed."

"Any suspicious-looking characters?" Dessa replied without looking up.

"You tell me," Mark said as he turned the screen to show Pamela Darah entering the building at 6 p.m.

"Who are we looking at?" Myrna asked. Mark froze the picture,

"That's Pamela Darah."

"The same woman on the men's computers?" Dessa remarked.

"One in the same," answered Mark with his Jamaican accent.

"What about Libra's phone?" Myrna replied, measured.

"Both phones had some steamy text messages and a long list of female names and numbers."

"How soon can we get that list of names?"

"Here you go," Mark said, handing Myrna half a dozen pieces of paper.

"Thanks, Mark, you're awesome!"

Mark murmured under his breath.

"Love Presha man too much, presha me waan presha yu pum…" Dessa knit her brow.

"Did you say something?" Mark's shoulders jumped.

"No ma'am." Dessa laughed to herself, not letting on that she understood every word he said. They stepped outside, and Myrna angled toward her partner.

"OK, what did he say this time?"

"He wants to pressure your vajayjay."

"Mine," she reacted,

"Why not yours?"

"Trust me, it's you."

"Why don't you just tell him that you're Jamaican?" Dessa shook her head, laughing.

"And let him know that I can understand every word he says; this way is much more fun."

The two left feeling optimistic that they were finally following a good lead. They hadn't been long at their desk when a call came in about a man who had been found dead near the parliament buildings.

Upon arrival at the scene, the ladies met a tall, silver-haired man, a seasoned investigator named Roy Brown.

"Who called you?" he asked defensively.

"This case is connected to the one I'm currently investigating."

"Says who?"

Myrna turned toward the uniforms clustered near the body. They talked over one another.

"stumbling drunk."

"Same old Crescent."

"Man couldn't hold his liquor."

Larry Crescent, his name alone drew a few eye rolls. The man had been hauled in more times than she could count for drunk and disorderly. Up close, the toll was carved into him: cheeks sagging and mottled, broken capillaries across his nose, skin the grayish yellow of a liver long at war. He looked twice his age. The stench of rum clung to him so thick the winter air didn't stand a chance against it.

"Alcohol poisoning," one of the officers muttered.

Too easy, Myrna crouched, letting her eyes travel the body, the ground, the small details that never lied. Something in the scene felt off, too arranged, too clean for the chaos Crescent usually left in his wake. She'd seen deaths like this before, wrapped in the disguise everyone expected. A drunk who'd finally drunk himself to death, except he hadn't.

Crescent was just like the others. Someone had turned him into another message, another riddle waiting to be cracked.

4

Bittersweet

Santana Osbourne rose early Wednesday morning, moving through the motions like a woman in someone else's body. She made breakfast, hands trembling as she buttered toast and poured juice, and readied her children in silence. When they were gone from the kitchen, she sat on the edge of her bed, half-dressed, her gaze fixed on nothing, her thoughts scattered like leaves in the wind. Her youngest daughter appeared quietly at her side, small fingers buttoning the blouse, smoothing the fabric, guiding her mother as though afraid she might break.

Downstairs, the car waited with its door open, swallowing the early light. Santana wore a long, dark purple skirt and a white blouse, the closest thing to mourning attire she owned, since anything black in her closet was too short, too tight, or too revealing for the day ahead.

The drive to the church seemed far too short, as if time itself had conspired against her. Outside the Presbyterian church, a cluster of Charles's friends gathered on the stone steps, their voices low, their eyes shifting toward her as she approached. She found it bitterly ironic; this man, who had never set foot in a pew, never spoken of God except in curses, now had a holy send-off.

Inside, the scent of polished wood and wilted lilies pressed against her. Words floated around her, tributes, condolences, voices breaking, but they slipped away as quickly as they came. Faces blurred; names vanished. In the haze of grief and disbelief, Santana couldn't even remember who had been there, only the echo of footsteps in the aisle and the weight of eyes she could not meet.

Finally, it was time to go to the gravesite. Myrna stood at the edge of the roadway near the cemetery, the gravel crunching under her shoes each time she shifted her weight. She had been waiting for Dessa for over an hour, the autumn air carrying the faint scent of turned earth and wilted flowers. The mourners' dark clothing fluttered lightly in the wind. From where she stood at the edge of the crowd, Myrna scanned the faces and whispers, piecing together the man Charles Libra had been. A few men on the edge of the crowd chuckled "Ganja Man" under their breath, the nickname slipping out the way old habits do, casual and familiar, as if they'd been calling him that his whole life. She'd heard his laugh in old recordings, big, booming, the kind that made people forget the smoke he was dealing on the side.

Myrna counted them in her head, three with Santana, a couple outside, maybe more if whispers were true. Near the back, two women avoided each other's eyes, each holding a child with the same wide, startled gaze. Myrna didn't need a family tree to understand the pattern he'd left behind. All the women looked tired, practiced, like they'd learned long ago not to expect anything more than fleeting charm, false promises, and endless excuses from men like him. One man in the crowd wore a faded DJ Libra T-shirt, the kind sold for twenty dollars outside backyard parties. Another kept glancing around nervously, the way men do when they know the police might recognize them from old mistakes. Libra's world was here, loud, tangled, and standing in front of her.

Myrna shifted her weight; gravel crunched under her shoe. 'Men like him,' she thought, 'they don't just make enemies. They manufacture them.' Her mind drifted back to the airport, the way Santana's suitcase slipped from her hand before the words were even out of Myrna's mouth. The shock, the half-step backward, the whisper of "no" caught in her throat. Myrna had reached for her, hating the role she had to play but knowing it spared Santana something far worse.

Santana Osbourne had the kind of beauty that drew glances and a presence that kept people at a distance. Her skin was a soft golden-brown shade of raw honey, poetically catching the light; a blend of her Black mother's warmth and her white father's sharp-boned elegance. High cheekbones framed a face that rarely smiled but was always observant. Her eyes, a pale hazel with flecks of green, could cut through pretence, as if she'd learned long ago how to read lies without a word. Her curls, thick and stubborn, were usually swept into a tight bun or braided down her back. She didn't wear much makeup, just a bold lip on the days she wanted to remind herself who she was.

Santana moved with quiet confidence, protecting her children from the news, a confidence born of knowing she'd survived worse than judgment. She raised three children on grit and instinct. Santana sold used cars. Her clothes were practical and sharp, fitted jeans, button-downs, and clean sneakers, but she could carry herself like a woman walking a red carpet, even when stepping out of a rusted-out Civic.

Life with Libra had taught her to keep her heart behind a locked door. He was charm and chaos wrapped in smoke and dreadlocks. She used to love him, back before the third lie, the second affair, and the first time she had to explain away his absence to the kids. Santana didn't cry easily, but when she did, it was in private, silent, behind locked bathroom doors. Now, with Charles gone and secrets surfacing like oil on water, she was done playing quiet. She wasn't afraid of cops, but she didn't trust them either. She knew how quickly people judged the woman left behind. But she had her kids to think about. Her survival didn't come with apologies.

Santana had reacted just as expected. It wasn't long after that that she was removed from the suspect list. Simms had been laid up with the flu, so Myrna had been on her own for a week. Myrna turned her head to notice a woman dressed in full black. She wore black stockings with four-inch heels. Her dress, which landed just at her knees, was accompanied by a broad-brimmed black hat with a veil. This woman was now coming toward Myrna, who was quite surprised to see that it was her partner, Dessa Simms.

"What the hell is with this get-up?" she asked.

"I thought that I could mingle in the crowd a little to get some info."

"Mingle, Simms, it's a funeral, not a party."

"Yeah, maybe it wasn't such a good idea after all; these shoes are killing me."

"So is that why you're so late?" Myrna, easing back on her heel.

"I stopped at the church service, but I got nothing."

"Simms, you're an enigma," Myrna responded with a slight

chuckle. She couldn't help thinking how naive Dessa was for a detective.

The two detectives looked up to observe a woman far off in the background on the other side of the cemetery. She wasn't dressed for the funeral, attired in jeans and a dark blue shirt. She stared curiously at the crowd gathered to say goodbye to Charles Libra. Simms and Watkis took notice and decided to investigate further. They snuck up on the woman, the two moving quickly, sliding their arms near her sides while she kept both arms tightly crossed over her chest, watching intently.

Simms identified her as Pamela Darah from the photograph they'd obtained.

"Permit me to introduce myself, Detective Watkis, and my partner here is Detective Simms." Pamela tried to get away, but the officers had a firm hold.

"Let's go downtown, shall we?" Dessa said with authority.

By the time the hearse pulled away, Pamela was already in their custody. Simms asked if Darah knew either Libra or Johnson, to which she answered:

"Libra? Johnson? Never heard of them," Her fingers drummed faster, sharp little taps that didn't match the calm in her voice. Both men had her on their computers.

"What were you doing at the cemetery? Dessa insisted.

"Sometimes I like to go and watch the facial expressions, I'm an artist, you know."

Myrna leaned forward, badge still glinting on her lapel.

"We have your pictures on Libra's computer, and records of emails with Johnson. So don't give me any bullshit about watching faces for art."

Pamela's eyes narrowed, a smile twitching at her lips.

"Art is bullshit, Detective. That's why it sells. But sure, if you want to think I was sketching faces at a funeral, knock yourself out."

Dessa cut in, voice flat.

"So what were you doing there?" Pamela's tone sharpened, her words cracking like glass.

"Fine! I came to see the bastard in the ground. Wanted to make sure he wasn't gonna crawl back out."

Dessa blinked.

"You're glad?"

Pamela leaned forward, the veil of her sarcasm slipping just enough to show heat underneath.

"Glad? Honey, I'd dance on his coffin in the pouring rain if I could find the right shoes."

Myrna's jaw clenched.

"Why should we believe you?"

Pamela tilted her head, lips curling in defiance.

"Because liars usually want to convince you. Me? I don't care if you believe a word. Check the damn time of death, check my alibi. You'll see I didn't do it."

Myrna smirked,

"Well, it just so happens, we know exactly where you were."

Pamela snapped back.

"Then good. You already know I'm not your girl."

Dessa chuckled darkly.

"Funny, because you were seen in the same location where Johnson was found."

Pamela's eyes flashed.

"What location?"

Myrna smiled, sharp as a blade.

"Sportsplex, Merivale Road. Tuesday, February 22nd."

Pamela rolled her eyes.

"Of course. I go every Tuesday. Ask anyone. You think going to AA makes me a murderer?"

"The big deal," Myrna countered,

"Is, that's the night Harry Johnson was killed there."

Pamela's voice cracked, higher now.

"I don't know a thing about Harry's death!"

Dessa folded her arms.

"But you said you were glad he's dead,"

Pamela slapped the table with her palm.

"No! I said I'm glad Libra's dead. Harry? Harry was an idiot, but not my problem." Her chest rose and fell fast, the first real crack in her armour.

"Now, unless you've got proof, I want my lawyer." Myrna exchanged a look with Dessa; no arrest today, but they had her rattled.

In the window of the local appliance store, a wall of television screens glowed, their colours flickering across the sidewalk. On every screen, a poised news reporter stood in front of yellow police tape, her hair unmoving despite the breeze, her expression solemn but hungry for attention.

"...police are now calling the suspect the 'Tuesday Killer,'" she announced, the words crisp and deliberate, as though branding the murderer for the evening broadcast. "Investigators say the killer only strikes on Tuesdays."

Myrna stopped dead in her tracks. A hot flush climbed up her neck, flooding her face until her cheeks burned crimson. Her jaw clenched, and her eyebrows drew together like storm clouds on a collision course.

"Fuck!"

The word came out in a low, sardonic hum, tight and

controlled but shaking with rage.

"Who the hell leaked that information?"

The glass reflected her scowl at her, distorted by the curve of the TV screens, so she looked like she was glaring from every channel at once.

"I don't know," Dessa's voice tinged with genuine surprise. The two women exchanged a glance, both fully aware how this would look to Sergeant Moses, who already regarded their work with all the enthusiasm of a man staring at cold porridge. The steady hiss and hum of passing traffic filled the air. Myrna spun on her heel and, without warning, lashed out with her foot, striking the stop signpost with a sharp metallic clang. The pole shivered in its cement base, the vibration ringing in the summer heat. Now pacing, Myrna exhaled under her breath, words spilling out in fragments. Her irritation radiated like static electricity.

With her trademark observational humour, Dessa ambled toward the post, hands in her pockets. She crouched low, peering intently at the spot Myrna's shoe had landed. Myrna, noticing the odd movement, frowned.

"What the hell are you doing?"

"You kicked the shit out of this post," Dessa said, running her fingers along the metal as though examining a crime scene.

"I'm looking for the dent."

"You're not going to make me laugh," Myrna replied, though her lips betrayed her with the faintest twitch.

"Mi jus' a seh," Dessa continued, straight-faced, "Girl, if I prick you right now, bet you don't bleed one drop. Remind me never to cuss you off." That broke her. Myrna doubled over with laughter.

"You and your Jamaican sayings."

"Come on," Dessa said, brushing off her hands and straightening up.

"Let's get out of here." With the traffic still rumbling by, the two women turned away from the flickering TV screens and the dentless stop sign, heading off to check in with Dr. Festus once more.

Larry Crescent had been on a first-name basis with every beat cop in Ottawa. Five-nine, potbelly sagging where muscle used to be; a face once handsome, now chewed up by years of liquor. He was the kind of man who still called himself 'lucky' while pouring cheap rum into a chipped mug at noon.

Myrna couldn't fathom a motive for killing him. A washed-up drunk didn't make enemies, unless someone wanted him silenced for a reason he'd never live long enough to explain. Compared to the others, Crescent looked out of place in the pattern, messy where they were deliberate, accidental where they were staged. 'That's what gets me,' she thought, 'like whoever did this wanted to leave behind something bittersweet.'

Once again, Myrna and Dessa found themselves seated across from Dr. Festus in his damp, refrigerated office, the faint smell of formaldehyde clinging to the air. The hum of the fluorescent light above seemed louder than usual, as though even it was listening. Festus slid a thin folder toward them, his expression unreadable.

"About your latest victim, Larry Crescent."

Myrna edged forward, bracing herself for another grim revelation.

"He had arsenic in his system," Festus said evenly,

"and... something else." He adjusted his glasses, the lenses catching the sterile glare.

"Vogney's ground-up toenails were found in his stomach." Dessa's head snapped back slightly, eyes narrowing. Myrna's lip curled, her tone sharp.

"So, he was poisoned, just not with alcohol?"

"Correct," Festus replied, his voice low, almost clinical.

"And one more thing."

He opened the folder again and turned a glossy crime-scene photo toward them.

Myrna's gaze landed on it, and her stomach gave a small, involuntary twist. Etched in crude black ink across Larry's bare back was a cartoonish drawing of a donkey grinning widely—a jackass, smiling. Myrna studied it. It wasn't a message like before, not a puzzle. It was a mockery. The others had died in theatre; Crescent had been turned into a joke. The room seemed to tighten around them. Myrna's hands pressed flat on the desk, knuckles blanching, while Dessa stared at the image, her jaw tightening, silent thoughts racing.

"I have a theory about the killer, if you want to hear it."

"By all means," Dessa said.

"I believe the killer is an orphan … traumatic Tuesdays … you see, it all fits."

Festus adjusted his glasses with unnecessary drama, as if unveiling brilliance.

"What are you basing this on?" Dessa asked.

"Well, based on the invisibility of the crimes, I feel the killer is probably a recluse, someone people rarely notice, and the Tuesday thing is self-explanatory."

"If you say so," Dessa replied, voice flat as stone.

"What, you don't agree?" She shook her head.

"Not a ting nuh go so. This isn't a Garfield comic, man, don't plan murder cause Tuesday boring."

Myrna couldn't help but laugh,

"I don't think the case is quite solved just yet,"

"Well, I tried to help," said Festus with a sheepish smile.

"Leave the catching of criminals to us." Myrna walked out the door with her partner, still laughing.

Saturday afternoon was rainy for Vogney's funeral. He'd been cremated. At the service, there were many men from the company where he worked. His wife was grief-stricken, along with his five children. On the other side of the church, Dessa noticed two women with children who looked a lot like Vogney's boys. Both women were as bereaved as his wife. Dessa pointed this out to Myrna, and when the service was over, they followed the two women out to question them.

"Excuse me, my name is Myrna Watkis, Ottawa P.D. May we ask you a few questions?"

The first woman wasn't too receptive, Britney Rellik, a nurse with whom Vogney had been involved. She held on to her daughter's hand tightly as she pushed her to stand behind her. The second lady did not have a problem. She was quite forthcoming and confirmed that she'd been involved with Vogney. The child, she claimed, was also his, but Vogney's wife knew nothing about her. Her name was Elaine Justif. Elaine had worked for years at the same company as Vogney, as a secretary. Britney reluctantly admitted that she, too, had a child with Vogney and was quite perturbed to find that she wasn't Vogney's only extramarital affair. She explained how she and Vogney practically lived together, and he took great care of her and their child.

Myrna started to think; now there's a motive if I've ever heard one. She wondered just how much in the dark Mrs. Vogney truly was. The two girlfriends were also placed on the suspect list. They, too, had a motive to kill Vogney. Myrna just had to connect them to the other victims. Jacob Asher was also a person of interest. He was the next stop on Simms and Watkis's agenda.

They drove along the Ottawa Parkway on the way to the West End to question Jacob Asher. Jacob was an alpine-built man with dark brown hair. He was missing one finger on his right hand that he lost in a machine shop incident. As Simms approached the steps of Asher's west-end apartment, she noticed several children playing across the street. Watkis wasn't far behind as they stepped into the corridor. They were surprised to see Johnson's name on one of the mailboxes in the corridor.

They had not been able to check out Johnson's apartment, but he had been listed at another address. While there, the two decided to kill two birds with one stone. A flip of a coin decided that Johnson's apartment would be visited first. They knocked on the door number displayed on the mailbox, and were surprised when the door opened to reveal a young female in a wheelchair. Her skin was like a mocha latte, creamy and smooth. She looked beautiful. Her natural hair crowns her, coils, springing free with confidence.

"Can I help you?"

Anika asked enthusiastically. The officers presented their badges.

"What can I do for you, Miss Watkis?"

Dessa found herself stunned at the contrast of the woman before her and the asshole that was Harry Johnson. 'How could such a woman end up with such a prick?'

"Does a Harry Johnson live here?" asked Myrna.

"Yes, of course, he's my husband. Did something happen to

him?" Anika was now beginning to show concern.

"Mrs. Johnson, Myrna began, I'm sorry to have to tell you this, but your husband was found dead at work on April 29th. He had been deceased for nine weeks." The woman didn't react at all; she stood completely in shock. Finally, she began crying uncontrollably as though the news was slowly hitting her.

"That's over two months ago. No, Harry wouldn't have been at work; he took leave and went back to Watertown. He's in the Army. That can't be, I spoke with him a month ago, remember?" Simms tried to console her,

"Mrs. Johnson, please..."

"No!" she shouted.

"You've got the wrong Harry Johnson. It's a popular name."

Her face collapsed, eyes wide, mouth open, breath trembling like she couldn't stitch a full thought together. She reached blindly for the nearest counter, knuckles white. When her knees buckled slightly, Myrna made the call for a friend to stay with her. Johnson had lied to his wife about going into the army. Simms and Watkis couldn't wait to visit his other address.

Just down the hall, apt. 210, Jacob Asher answered the door in his underwear. Myrna's lip curled the instant she saw him, bare chest, banana in hand, zero shame. He chomped on the banana as if he hadn't eaten in months.

"What do you want?"

He said, with absolutely no manners. Once again, Simms and Watkis garnished their badges.

"I'm clean,"

"Relax," Dessa said, "we're here to investigate the murder of Harry Johnson."

Asher dropped the remains of his banana.

"Who, who'd you say?" Jacob asked in complete shock.

"Harry Johnson, we found your name on his computer," Dessa stepped back two steps. Jacob retreated to his living room, and the detectives followed.

"Me and Harry are good friends. I look out for his wife when he's..." Jacob lowered his head into his hands.

"Go on," Dessa said.

"Well, Harry plays around a lot, and when he goes to his other apartment, I make sure his wife is alright."

"She says she spoke with him a month ago, know anything about that?"

"He recorded his voice so I could play it; it made her happy." The ladies gave each other a look as if to say, Yeah, right!

"What about Charles Libra?" asked Myrna.

"Who?" Asher said again, sharply.

"You were found on his computer, also."

Dessa intently watched for a reaction.

"Yeah, I knew Charles Libra. I was bummed when I heard the news that he'd been murdered."

"Oh, really, Myrna interjected, what was your relationship with Charles?"

"Well, I used to get marijuana from him. I've got cancer, and the stuff helps. Are you going to arrest me for that?"

"No, we're more interested in apprehending the person who killed these men," Myrna continued.

"Well, I had no reason to kill either of them."

"We'll be in touch, said the officers as they walked away, taking along the recording.

They walked to the end of the hallway, beckoning toward Harry Johnson's other apartment. It was about half an hour until they arrived at the 12-storey apartment building on

Somerset St., downtown Ottawa. Upon arrival, they met with the landlord, a 35-year-old immigrant from Jamaica. Closing his office door quickly in an attempt to avoid them, told Dessa he had something to hide.

Slowly extending her elbow to nudge Myrna, Dessa raised her eyebrows and pushed her way into the room. Threatening him with a trip to the station seemed to work wonders as he admitted that he'd taken a bribe from Johnson to look the other way when this curly-haired redhead came to live with him, as she was not on the lease. He also confirmed Asher's story about Johnson being a womanizer. Johnson had a one-month deadline for each lady he brought to live with him.

Stella Monet was the kind of woman who didn't just enter a room; she draped herself across it. Pale skin with an olive cast, legs that went on forever, and platinum-blond hair that looked two days overdue for a dye job. She answered the door in a skin-tight, extremely short minidress. By now, she was well aware that Harry was dead and quite happy to cooperate. She invited them in. Her dress was red, her lips were redder, and her confidence clung to her like perfume. She knew exactly what she was doing and didn't give a damn if anyone liked it.

At first glance at the apartment, Myrna thought of only one word: cheesy. The apartment had been decorated with stereotypical furniture, like a heart-shaped bed. There was a lot of red, remote-controlled music, the heart-shaped bed and faded strategic lighting that went off and on when one clapped. A total contrast to Anika Johnson's home, everything in the apartment begged for secrecy and seduction.

The woman sat cross-legged, and Myrna could see the edge of her red underwear peeking out. 'Well, at least she's wearing one,' thought Myrna.

"How long have you been living here?" She asked. Stella moved with slow, deliberate precision; every step, every glance, premeditated like a stripper who knew the power of her body.

"About a month," Stella Monet responded proudly, tossing her head back.

"Were you aware that Harry Johnson had a wife?"

"Of course, I was aware that he was married, even though he denied it. There were signs, and men are idiots." Dessa is unable to hide her disgust.

"You didn't have a problem sleeping with another woman's husband?" Stella looked her straight in the eye with a little attitude and said.

"I needed a place to stay, and he treated me well, win-win.

"How long since you've seen Johnson?" Dessa asked.

"A few weeks or more?"

Myrna asked, puzzled,

"Why didn't you report him missing?"

"I assumed that he was with his wife at first, but realized that something was wrong when I didn't hear from him after a certain amount of time."

"And then?" She quickly raised and lowered her shoulders.

"Well, I figured that calling to report him missing was his wife's job." She got up and adjusted her dress.

"If you'll excuse me, I am on my way to work."

The two detectives walked out with her and went their separate ways. It was only a few seconds before Dessa exclaimed,

"Work!"

"Yeah, bet it involves a street or a pole," retorted Myrna. They had a good laugh, and Dessa headed home.

Today was the second Friday of the month, which meant that Myrna had a dinner date with her mother. Her mother greeted her with the same warm squeeze as always, pressing a kiss to her forehead before insisting she take the seat closest to the kitchen

"So I can feed you properly." She would say. The bread hadn't even hit the table before her mother's eyebrow arched.

"So... anyone special?"

"Mother, please. I would just like to enjoy our dinner."

"Myrna, you're not getting any younger, and I want grandchildren."

Myrna took a slow sip of her wine, avoiding her mother's hopeful eyes. Commitment was the last thing she had room for. By dessert, they'd hit the same wall as always, her mother's sigh, Myrna's half-smile, both accepting they wouldn't win tonight's round. Myrna went home, slept, but her mind didn't. Somewhere out there, the killer was wide awake.

5

First Kiss

Reflecting on the chaos left behind was fun. It was hell, waiting, anticipating the discovery of the first kiss. Finally, the game had begun; it was time to reach out and be cordially introduced.

Four I kissed, two will bleed,
two will beg, and one will lead.
The one who leads once looked away,
A quiet debt will now repay.
My dear detective, even you can see,
I've made it so bloody easy.
the idea of prison makes me frown,
I'm not cut out to be locked down.
so I shan't be going there,
since it's something I could never bare.
As for the boys, don't even waste a tear,
They earned their end. Let's make that clear.
I gave you clues, not because I'm kind
But because your brain's a step behind.

Connect the dots? You never could.
So I did it, like a killer should.
No need to roll in a tailspin,
I'm not afraid. You'll never win.

Kisses!

Myrna's stomach dropped as she reread the final word—'Kisses' scrawled in ink like a fingerprint. The page mocked her, smug in its stillness. Then she noticed where it lay: dead center on her desk, waiting as if it knew she would come. Her pulse spiked.

"Who the hell put this here?" Watkis's voice cracked like a whip across the room. No one looked up. Phones rang, keyboards clacked, conversations carried on as if a taunting message from a killer wasn't sitting in plain sight.

The door creaked. Simms strolled in, dropped her bag, and slid into the other half of their shared desk.

"What's up?" she asked, glancing from the paper to Myrna's stiff posture.

"Look at this," Watkis said, handing her the letter.

"What the hell!" Simms exclaimed.

"We need to get the handwriting analyzed."

"It's typed, Simms."

"Except for that one word." Myrna jabbed the page.

"Kisses. That's in ink!"

"Focus Watkis, you can't let this thing get to you."

"Alright, let's take it upstairs to the technicians."

"It'll be a good while before we get any results." The two officers left the hustle and bustle of the squad room to go upstairs and inform the tech team that they wanted the results by yesterday. Leaving the tech office, Simms and Watkis headed out into the field. Every board they revisited only deepened the silence; lines that should've connected ended bluntly, and clues circled the same void. The more they dug, the more the case slipped like smoke through their fingers.

The wing of the building that Johnson was found in had been locked off due to minor repairs pending. This individual must have been familiar with the building's intricacies, as well as Johnson's schedule. Watkis let out a slow breath, tapping the construction map with her pen.

"Someone knew this wing was empty... too well."

Simms flipped through the files, her brow tightening.

"All roads keep circling back to Pamela Darah. Whether we like it or not."

Libra's family was out of town, and the family's work schedule must also have been known. Reviewing the cases led both women to believe that the killer knew the men's personal lives, since Pamela Darah was the only connection found thus far. She would remain at the top of the list.

Right now, she was the only one who appeared to have the means and opportunity to kill Harry and Charles. However, there were a few more ladies on the list of persons of interest. First, Sue, the woman who may have been having an affair with Libra. Second, Vogney's wife. Third, Vogney's two baby mothers; fourth, Anika Johnson and finally, Stella Monet.

Watkis decided to find a way to tie the other two victims to Darah. First on the agenda was an in-depth look into Darah's background. A search warrant was obtained to search Darah's home. The search of Darah's home hadn't turned up much at first. Simms rifled through drawers, her frown deepening with each empty result.

"Clean. Too clean." A monogram tie with the initials E.V. was found in one of her drawers. Watkis thought for sure that E.V. stood for Elias Vogney. At first glance, everything sat exactly where it belonged, almost too neatly. Nothing jumped out, nothing screamed for attention.

A further look made Darah's home seem strange.

Her kitchen was obsessively organized: bottles were alphabetized, labels faced forward, and everything was aligned to the inch. The bathroom gleamed as if it had never been touched.

The place was completely spotless. On Pamela's bed sat a doll, propped neatly against pillows. At first glance, it was ordinary. But a closer look revealed scorch marks hidden along its seams, and its face, disturbingly, was Pamela's own in miniature.

Later that day, Watkis and Simms checked in on the Vogney evidence. Valdez, with black hair sticking up like she hadn't slept, hunched over a workbench, protective goggles in place.

Valdez set her tools down and pushed the goggles up onto her head.

"I just finished processing Vogney's vehicle. The brake line was deliberately severed, clean cut. And the air vent, rigged with pepper spray. It would have triggered after the engine warmed and the fan kicked in."

"Clever," Dessa said, almost impressed. Myrna exhaled sharply, shaking her head.

"That explains the burns Festus found. And it means the killer was thinking three steps ahead."

Dessa folded her arms.

"Cold-blooded. They wanted him blind and choking before they even laid hands on him."

Valdez raised a brow.

"You asked me for science, Detectives. Science says this wasn't sloppy. Whoever you're chasing knows exactly what they're doing."

Myrna adjusted her holster.

"Thanks, Valdez. Keep us posted. Simms, we've got Asher at the station. Time to go."

Jacob Asher sat fidgeting with a pen he'd found inside his pocket. It had been a good forty-five minutes since he'd been placed in that small room with four walls and a table. Asher fidgeted, twisting the pen so hard it clicked against his knuckles. Every few seconds, he glanced at the door, hoping, failing, to hide the nerves tightening his jaw. The door opened.

"Good morning, Detective Dessa Simms. For our records, state your name."

"Jacob Asher."

"At any time during this interview, if you require a lawyer, just say so." Asher nodded.

"Ok," Simms continued.

"Seems you're quite the gentleman. All the people questioned in your building say you take very good care of Mrs. Johnson."

"Yeah, well, somebody has to."

"You care about her, huh?" Dessa leaned in.

"Care enough to kill for her?"

"Seriously, that's the best you can do, kill for Anika?"

"Harry was my best friend, we go way back. Yeah, he was an asshole, but he was still my friend." Simms took a folder she had and opened it.

"Three weeks before Johnson was found dead, you were photographed buying a torch. I have witnesses that say they've seen you with an I.V. mechanism, and finally, there's the access you have to embalming fluid at the funeral home where you work."

"So what? I use an IV for my illness. Remember, I have cancer. The torch was a gift for a friend's birthday."

"What about the embalming fluid? You know he was pumped up with the stuff."

"Well, not by me. I wish I could catch the son-of-a-bitch that killed him."

"Trust me, you'd better hope you catch him first."

"Harry was my boy, man. We've been friends since he first came to Canada." Asher buried his head in his hands as he sobbed uncontrollably. When Simms saw his face crumple and the sobs break free, she exhaled sharply, damn, wrong angle. On the bright side, she had concrete evidence to nail Pamela Darah, who was on her way into the station.

6

Silver Foil

Pamela Darah stepped into a cavernous waiting area, the air heavy with the scent of disinfectant and stale coffee. The room buzzed with restless energy, heels tapping against scuffed linoleum, voices murmuring in anxious fragments, the metallic clang of a cell door slamming shut somewhere down the hall. Her chest tightened, each breath shallow, as if the walls themselves were inching closer.

Fists curling at her sides, she forced her chin up and walked a measured path past the holding cells, where shadowed faces pressed against bars, their eyes following her like silent accusations. She kept her gaze fixed forward, unwilling to meet them.

At last, she reached a narrow doorway and was ushered into a cramped interview room. This time, she wasn't alone. Waiting for her, calm and deliberate, was one of Ottawa's most formidable legal minds, Johnathan Karamel, a presence that seemed to command the space before either of them spoke.

He was known for his ruthlessness and cunning. He very rarely lost a case. Watkis already knew of his reputation and was reminded this morning by the D.A., Simone Mansfield, not to leave any stones unturned before making an arrest. Simms sat opposite Karamel, shoulders squared, while Myrna took the chair closest to the door, file in hand.

"We can connect your client to each of the victims," Watkis began.

"No, that's not possible," Pamela answered.

"Remain silent," Karamel interjected.

"Detective, just what is the evidence that you have?"

"Just as I said," Watkis continued. "Ms. Darah's name and image were found on both Mr. Libra's and Mr. Johnson's computers. We found a monogrammed tie in one of your drawers with the initials E.V."

"What, what tie?" Darah asked in denial.

"I said, be quiet!" Karamel, now raising his voice.

"Detective, you haven't proven a thing. Stop wasting our time." Simms stood up.

"You haven't heard the best part. Larry Crescent was a part of your AA group up until about a week before he died."

"Funny thing, Pamela. Your name keeps showing up where bodies do." Watkis interjected.

"I know dead people. Doesn't mean I killed them." Karamel got up, smiled smugly, and motioned to his client to follow him out of the interview room. As the door clicked shut behind them, Simms blew out a tight breath.

"Give me an hour with her alone, she'd crack."

Myrna stared at the empty chair Pamela had left behind. The warrant in her hand suddenly felt too thin.

"Yeah," she said quietly.

"But today the lawyer walks her out, and we just get to watch."

Myrna flipped through Libra's file for what felt like the hundredth time, pages already soft at the edges from her thumb. She stopped at the crime-scene photo, the condom wrapper glinting in the corner of the bedroom photo.

"The wrapper was on the floor," she groused, tapping it with her pen.

"But at autopsy, the condom shows up on him. That means it was used between the two."

Dessa leaned back in her chair, arms folded.

"Which tells us what we already suspected: he knew his killer. Trusted her enough to get that close. She played him, made him think it was sex, not death waiting."

Myrna exhaled, eyes narrowing at the photo.

"She didn't need brute force. She just needed him comfortable, distracted long enough to slip the drug in."

"Classic honey trap," Dessa said, grimacing.

"Only this time, the prize wasn't his wallet."

They sat with that for a moment, the board looming over them with photos and timelines, each clue pushing them closer and yet never close enough.

Larry Crescent went into the ground on a gray morning, the church air heavy as wet wool. His father buckled at the coffin, held up by two sons, while a sister screamed his name until her voice cracked raw.

Watching Crescent's father fold over the coffin, Myrna felt a sour question tug at her: how did a man with this many arms ready to hold him still choose the bottle instead? Then she thought of silver foil; wrapped secrets, shiny on the outside, rotten underneath, just like the lies unravelling around this case.

The line of mourners snaked long and sincere, hands

squeezed, shoulders clapped and whispered.

"he was good at heart."

Yet she'd still seen him sleeping under bus shelters. Whatever help had been offered, somewhere along the way, he'd stepped around it. His ex-wife never showed. When Myrna asked around, the answers came in fragments.

"Sandra? Thought she died in a wreck years back."

"No, no, she left him long before that. Man wouldn't put the bottle down."

"No kids together," someone said, "but a grown daughter from before." His daughter stood at the graveside like she was bracing against a storm, her mother hovering close, the diamond on her hand loud and unapologetic. By the time the coffin was lowered, Myrna's notebook was still mostly blank. This visit was more about watching than learning.

A week later, Johnson's mother leaned trembling over the coffin, her frail hand brushing the scorched skin of his face before breaking into sobs.

Johnson's mother's sobs still echoed as Myrna quietly photographed the guest book on her way out. Neither detective spoke. The only thing moving in the room was grief, heavy, slow, settling over every bowed head. Myrna lowered the camera, feeling like each click was an intrusion.

The two officers revisited the technician's office to inquire about the letter. They didn't understand at first why Mark, the head technician, was laughing so hard.

"Handwriting?" Mark chuckled, spinning in his chair.

"That's not handwriting. It's an app." He tapped a key, and the word *kisses* bloomed across his screen in a dozen different fonts.

"Click, print, done."

Dessa swore under her breath. Myrna pinched the bridge of her nose. Another lead gone cold.

"Every damn time," Myrna let the words slip out.

"We chase ghosts, and all we get is fonts."

Dessa tried to lighten it.

"Hey, at least we know the killer's got Wi-Fi."

Neither laughed. The silence between them was sharp enough to cut.

Thursday morning, Simms and Watkis went to trace the social insurance number of Sandra Davidson. They wanted to know if she was indeed deceased. The clerk squinted at the screen, then at the form.

"Sandra Davidson... yeah. Deceased. Four years ago. Car accident."

Simms frowned.

"Four years? Thought they'd split long before that."

"Two years prior," Myrna said quietly, scanning the dates. He still fell apart after she died. Even from a distance, some people hold the last bit of you together."

The stack of closed files on Simms's desk had grown thicker than the open ones. She slammed one shut.

"Another dead end." Myrna didn't bother answering; the tension in her jaw said enough. Simms remembered the porn site that had been on three of the men's computers. They decided to visit the company that posted the site 'BrownSuga.com.' To get a list of people the men interacted with, they needed a warrant.

Judge Stone signed off without much argument, sliding the warrant back with a dry,

"You always bring me the fun ones, Watkis." She took it with a nod; his signature was as good as a vote of confidence.

By the next afternoon, the paper was in her hand, crisp and official, and she headed straight for BrownSuga.com.

The place smelled faintly of expensive perfume and over-heated electronics. Behind the glossy reception desk, a young woman in a too-tight blouse froze mid-keystroke when Myrna slid the warrant across the counter. No argument, just a thin, professional smile and a quiet,

"One moment, please."

Myrna watched the monitor reflect in the receptionist's glasses as fingers typed slowly, almost grudgingly. The list that finally emerged was neat, precise, and damning. There it was: three names she knew all too well, each tied to a single woman. Suga Plum.

Her real name, Belinda Ventures, sat buried in the account file like a splinter under skin. A few months with the company, yet her schedule read like a high-class chessboard of routine. Vogney had her locked in every Monday and Wednesday. Libra owns Tuesdays and Thursdays. Johnson took Fridays and Saturdays.

Six days a week. Same faces, same patterns. Belinda was more than just busy; she was *kept*. And Myrna couldn't help but wonder who was keeping her, and why three dead men had all been on her calendar.

Her hips swayed with the sound of a noisy drum. Never entreating, always over-promising. But her eyes, dark and sharp, scanned the room with the speed of someone who had learned early to measure exits, threats, and opportunities. She dropped into the chair across from the detectives, one long leg crossed over the other, daring them to blink first.

"So," she purred,

"We gonna talk business, or you just brought me in here to

stare?"

Dessa's voice hardened.

"Business. Vogney, Libra, Johnson."

Belinda's lips curved into a smile that was all teeth.

"Men pay for company. It's a lonely world. I provide a service, call it therapy with sequins." She leaned in, lowering her voice.

"And don't pretend Ottawa saints don't tune in after midnight."

Myrna scribbled, unimpressed.

"Did you ever meet any of them off-screen?"

Belinda's laugh was quick, but there was no music in it.

"No. That's against the rules. I follow rules." Her nails tapped the metal table, one-two-three, like she was holding herself together by rhythm. Then softer, almost too quiet to catch:

"You follow rules, you survive."

The detectives exchanged a glance because, for one heartbeat, Belinda wasn't performing.

When Belinda walked out, Simms exhaled through her teeth. "You buy that?"

"Not for a second," Myrna said, eyes on the closed door.

"But until we get something solid, she walks."

Just as they were about to leave for the day, a tumbling sound roared from the Sergeant's office. That was when Sergeant Moses called them in and introduced Patrick Jones, a new face, a new theory, and new tension.

"This is Patrick Jones. He's a pro-filer from the Nepean division." Mr. Jones stood up with his arm extended. Myrna shook his hand. Simms just nodded her head. Both women knew what was coming and were not to protest in any way.

"Since you two nitwits can't seem to come up with anything, I've asked Mr. Jones here to help out." Without saying another word, Simms and Watkis walked out of the office, followed by Patrick. The three sat at Simms and Watkis' desks. Mr. Jones began to speak.

"I've been to the crime scenes and reviewed all the case files, and I think I can give you a clear visual of who this killer is."

"Go ahead," Myrna responded, anticipating failure.

"First of all," Jones continued with confidence, "she has had a relationship with all four men. All the killings were personal. There's some significance to the chocolate kisses being left at each crime scene."

"Wait a minute, Dessa responded, Johnson had some in his jacket pocket, but nothing like that showed up at the other crime scenes."

"I beg to differ, chocolate kisses were found embedded in the pages of the owner's manual inside the glove compartment of Vogney's vehicle."

"If you look closely at Libra's crime scene photos, you'll notice some kisses in the vase on top of the toilet tank."

Myrna shook her head vigorously.

"There was nothing in there but some shiny stones."

"There were stones, yes, but the shiny ones were chocolate kisses in silver foil. And it's not random the kisses, those aren't just trophies; they're messages, ritualistic and personal."

"What about Crescent?" Myrna cleared her throat.

"Among the garbage next to where he was found, a brown paper bag that once contained a cheap bottle of gin crumpled up with a few chocolate kisses inside. There was also a note which read:

> One kiss for silence.
> One kiss for shame.
> Another for those who know my name.
> Sweet as sin, I leave them still—
> Not for love, but for the thrill.
> – Kisses!

"Wait a minute," the two detectives were aghast. "How did we miss this?" Dessa said

"Well, it's what I do; I have a passion for details."

"So what's the significance of the chocolate kisses?" Dessa asked.

"Honestly, I'm not sure, it's personal though. It means something to our killer, one thing is certain: it demonstrates her arrogance."

"Each bag was opened, which means she must have handled them. Possibly even eaten from them."

"She is very self-assured. Each scene is controlled; she wants to be noticed, taunting, maybe even flirting with you." Myrna was surprised.

"With me?"

"You and Simms. Leaving kisses like breadcrumbs, and then the letters, that's the real conversation. You're being drawn in!"

"Is that it?" Dessa thought to herself. 'Except for the chocolate, we had pretty much figured out the rest.'

He went on,

"This killer is highly intelligent, and she's not just killing. She's proving something." Myrna sits, frustrated.

"So what is she trying to prove?" Jones slants forward.

"That she's always one step ahead. That she knows your patterns, maybe even your past." Dessa looked at him curiously,

"You think we know her?"

"I think she knows you."

"Thanks for the info, Myrna said, I'm glad you pointed out that stuff about the chocolate. We overlooked it. Frankly, the rest of the info. is not new to us, though." Mr. Jones didn't say it, but he thought they were being ungrateful. When Jones finally left, Myrna stared at the board again. Same faces, same lines, nothing new.

"We already knew she was bold, already knew she touched every one of them. He just gave it better packaging."

Myrna began sifting through each name on the list. The first person to zero in on was Sue. They had finally tracked her down. Sue walked like every sidewalk owed her rent, hips swinging, chin high, eyes daring anyone to look away first. She wore what Dessa called hooker shoes with see-through mesh shorts and a tank top. She had a 40-size cleavage, so everything protruded from left to right, her hot-pink halter top glinting with sequins that caught the streetlight like flirtation.

Gold hoops grazed her shoulders every time she tossed her braids, which she did often, like punctuation. Her stilettos clicked with the rhythm of someone who'd long since decided pain was no excuse for silence. Even in a crowded room, Sue didn't enter; she arrived. And when she smiled, it was slow and carnivorous, like she knew your secrets before you did.

"What can I do for you, officers?" she asked innocently.

Myrna flashed her badge.

"We're investigating Charles Libra's death."

Sue rolled her eyes.

"And? You think I put him in the ground? Please. Charles was drama wrapped in dreadlocks. If I wanted that much headache, I'd marry a lawyer."

Dessa settled with her arms drawn across her front, gaze steady.

"Your name was in his phone."

Sue smirked.

"Yeah, we had a thing. Six months. Ended when his woman caught wind. He kept calling, though. Wanted me like rent money, always due."

Dessa unfolded her arms.

"So he was your dealer."

Sue snorted.

"Dealer's a big word. He tossed me a bag now and then. Sometimes for cash, sometimes for... incentive."

Myrna's pen scratched the page.

"When was the last time you saw him?"

"Two weeks before he croaked. Sold me some weed. Best part about Charles, he was reliable for that, at least." She shrugged.

"Charm, lies, and good shit. That's his legacy."

Myrna drew her arms tight, posture sharpening.

"You do remember we're cops, right?"

"And you do remember I don't care, right? I sold him nothing; he sold me plenty." A pregnant pause, and then Sue folded her arms loosely, a nervous barrier.

"He was charming, cocky, but charming. Didn't want commitment, just control; he collected secrets like trophies."

Dessa raised her eyebrows.

Myrna stepped forward.

"Did you see him the week he died?"

"Nope. And if I had, trust me, you'd know, Charles didn't shut up about anything." Sue cinched her arms tight, shoulders rising defensively.

"But let me guess, you think every woman who slept with

him wanted him dead. Truth is, most of us just wanted him gone."

"And you're sure you haven't been to his apartment recently?"

"Dead sure. Last time I was there, he got rough, paranoid, and swore I was talking to cops. Tried to set me up. I walked, never looked back." Dessa exchanged a glance with Myrna,

"Did he ever mention anyone following him?"

"Enemies?"

"Always thought someone was watching, said he 'felt heat.' Me? I figured it was the weed talking. Charles lied like he breathed."

Myrna nodded, putting away her notebook.

"Thanks, Sue. That helps. You'll be available if we need anything else?" Sue nods.

"Yeah. I want this behind me, believe it or not. Charles was a lot of trouble, but no one deserves to die like that."

The detective moved to walk away.

"One more thing," Dessa turned back.

"You know a Harry Johnson?"

"Harry, Harry Johnson, oh, he used to work at that security place with Charles. I used to hang around there. Harry wanted me first, but I love a tall, brown-skinned black man." Breathing heavily, "Charles had my eye from the beginning."

"Can you tell us where you were at the time Charles was killed?"

"Oh, who knows, girl, I don't keep track of that shit. I'm a busy woman, period." To Myrna, Sue's words tumbled out fast and carelessly, skipping over timelines and details like they were optional. She joked about cheating and weed with the same shrug she might use over a missed bus.

"We're not done with her," Myrna said once Sue was out of earshot.

"A woman like that doesn't just walk away clean because she shrugs."

Simms nodded in agreement.

"Even if she wanted Libra gone, how the hell does that stretch all the way to Vogney and Crescent?"

That was the part that wouldn't settle: too many bodies, one woman with a grudge, and gaps big enough to drive a cruiser through.

7

Kisses Too Close

The next day, detectives arrived at the busy police division shortly after finishing their interview with Darah. They'd barely dropped into their chairs when Myrna froze. A small bag of chocolate kisses sat dead center on her desk, a folded note propped against it like a calling card.

> You almost had me in your snare.
> I felt your shadow in the air.
> But close, dear Detective Simms, isn't quite—
> I slipped away into the night.
> Enjoy the chocolate, dark and sweet,
> a gift your victim couldn't eat.
> —Kisses!

Myrna squinted at the note, her lip a hard line.

"Arogant son of a bitch thinks this is a game!"

Dessa drummed her fingers on the table, sharp taps betraying her impatience.

"Or it's no coincidence. These notes show up right after Darah's interview, same timing, same perfume."

Myrna lifted the page to her nose. A faint trace of perfume lingered, Darah's brand, unless her memory failed her. Too neat, too easy. Circumstantial at best.

"Well, it's enough to start building a case."

Myrna didn't argue. Pamela's name sat closest to the center of their board, circled twice. But the other names were still there, pinned and waiting. She wasn't ready to pull any of them down.

Elaine Justif sat rigidly at her horseshoe desk, typing briskly on the laptop provided to her. Now and then, she would glance at her daughter's picture and recognize her father's eyes. Her eyes were dry, red at the rims, like someone who'd used up every tear and refused to make more. She looked up to see the two detectives coming toward her.

"Now what?" she said to herself.

"Good morning, Miss Justif. We were hoping you could answer a few questions for us."

"Do I have a choice?" she said, tossing her brown hair back.

"How long were you involved with Mr. Vogney?" Her long, thin face angled downward, brown eyes blinking. Miss Justif did not answer.

"I'm guessing," Myrna continued, "your daughter is about five."

"Yeah, we had been going on and off for about six years. I got pregnant not long after we met."

"So, when was the last time you saw him alive?"

"About a week before, he had to go out of town for work. He was back about a day before it happened."

"Does he have any enemies here at work or anywhere, for that matter?"

"Elias was well known for his womanizing. I'm sure he made an abundance of enemies over the years."

"What about you and him?" Dessa asked.

"Were you on good terms?"

"Lately, we were not on speaking terms. I think he was finally realizing that I was done with the relationship. He wasn't ever going to leave his wife, and I had to get on with my life." Shuffling papers, Elaine turned in her chair. A burn scar marked her wrist. Dessa noticed it immediately.

"Hey, where did you get that?" Elaine gave a thin smile, tugging down her sleeve.

"Burnt myself in the kitchen. Happens." The two detectives left after taking a few pictures. Out in the hallway, Dessa rubbed her own wrist thoughtfully.

"That scar doesn't look like a frying pan to me."

"No," Myrna agreed. "More like someone grabbed hot metal under a hood."

After a brutal overnight shift, Britney Rellik only wanted her bed until a hard knock shattered the quiet of her townhouse. She opened the door, still wearing her powder-blue scrubs, the faint scent of antiseptic clinging to her. Her curly raspberry hair, loosened from a hastily tied bun, whipped across her cheek in the early morning wind. Standing on her porch were two detectives, their badges catching the pale light.

"Good morning, Miss Rellik, may we come in?" Dessa's tone was polite, but it carried the weight of something more. Britney's eyes narrowed.

"Look, I just got off work, and I'm dead tired."

"It'll only take a moment," Dessa replied smoothly. With

a reluctant step back, Britney allowed them inside. The detectives entered the compact but well-kept townhouse, where the faint aroma of brewed coffee still lingered in the air. Sunlight spilled across a cozy living room, soft cream walls, a bookshelf neatly organized, and a gray throw blanket folded over the arm of the sofa.

"Nice place you have here," Dessa said, her gaze scanning more than just the décor. Britney gestured toward the couch.

"Please, have a seat. As I said, I'm tired, so let's get to the point." Her arms folded, and she remained standing, as if keeping the conversation on a strict clock.

Dessa took the lead, her voice even but probing, while Myrna let her eyes wander over the small townhouse. Britney dropped into an armchair, shoulders sagging, fingers worrying the seam of the cushion like it held the words she wouldn't say.

"The last time I saw Elias was the day before he died." Dessa took out her notebook.

"How long were you and Vogney together?"

"We'd been together for six years," she said, her tone flat, though the faint tremor in her voice betrayed a ripple of something unspoken. Six years, thought Dessa. That's a long time to stick by a man like him. He was a real piece of work. She went on.

"Yes, he was an asshole and a womanizing prick, but Elias had always supported his children financially," a fact she had stated, like a grudging credit in an otherwise damning review.

"Yeah, I knew about his wife, but that other woman…Elaine." She turned her head in a futile attempt to mask her contempt.

"The minute I saw her little girl at the funeral, I knew. Same curly hair, olive skin, same age as my Jenna." Dessa and Myrna looked at each other as if to read each other's minds. Shifting focus, Myrna showed Birtney photographs of the victims.

"Do you recognize these men?"

"I met Johnson once or twice at the hospital. I don't know the other two."

Myrna's attention was snagged on something in the room. The mantel, the shelves, every wall frame showed only Britney and her daughter, as if Vogney had never existed.

The space itself was modest: a narrow galley kitchen branching off the living room, its countertops neat but cramped; a small dining table tucked against the wall, barely enough room to move without brushing past something.

The statement seemed to hang in the air, unanswered questions buzzing just under its surface. By the time the detectives stepped back out into the daylight, they felt the weight of the long day pressing into their bones. Dessa headed to the West Indian restaurant on the corner, lured by the promise of curried chicken and rice. Myrna's craving was simpler: pasta at home, eaten in silence, while she replayed Britney's answers in her mind.

The next morning, the air outside the squat, brick building that housed the porn site was thick with exhaust and the faint tang of last night's rain. Myrna and Dessa stepped onto the sidewalk, their minds still sifting through the stale stench of the offices upstairs. They were halfway to their unmarked sedan when a sudden roar of an engine shattered the street's hum. An emerald-green Toyota Tercel screeched around the corner, jumped the curb, and lunged at them like a predator.

"Move!" Dessa shouted, shoving Myrna sideways as the car lunged at them.

Myrna dove sideways, hitting the pavement hard. Her brain snagged on one wild thought: *they want us silenced, just like* the others. Dessa's momentum carried her into a reeking pile of black garbage bags, their plastic crinkling beneath her weight. The car tore past, clipping the corner of a mailbox before vanishing down the block. Both women scrambled to their feet, breath ragged, adrenaline pounding in their ears. No glimpse of the driver. No license plate. Only the echo of a revving engine faded into the distance. Myrna's pulse thudded in her ears. Cars didn't just hop sidewalks by accident, not aimed that straight, not that close.

By mid-afternoon, they were back at their desks, the near miss only sharpening their resolve. A fax slid through, details on Crescent's ex-wife. According to the report, she'd died in a single-vehicle accident, her car had lost control on a coastal road and plunged over a cliff. But what snagged Myrna's attention was the gap: two missing years. No bills, no purchases, no addresses, no trace of life at all, a carbon ghost. The paperwork said 'accident,' but Myrna's instincts said otherwise.

Crescent's sister leaned back in her chair, eyes fixed on some distant point.

"He was always a drinker," she said. "But Sandra didn't know. Not at first. By the time she figured it out, her hair was falling out in clumps from the stress."

She shook her head.

"She dragged him to meetings, doctors, pastors, you name it. He'd sober up for a week, then disappear all day and come back smelling like a bar floor. Lost jobs, lost friends... and once he started hitting her, that was it. She packed up and left."

The timeline nagged at Myrna: years of silence before Sandra's supposed crash.

"She knew the others, too?" Myrna pressed.

"All of them," the sister sighed. "Worked with Vogney at the juice place. Libra's woman? That's Sandra's sister. And she dated Johnson before she met Larry. Small world, I guess."

Later, back at the board, Myrna dragged Sandra's name to the center, threads suddenly everywhere.

"She touches all four," Myrna said quietly.

"If she's alive, she's our bridge."

Dessa nodded once.

"Then we stop asking if, we prove it."

As Dessa looked down at her arm, she noticed a slight scratch that came from diving away from that emerald green vehicle.

"We've got to catch the son-of-a-bitch that tried to kill us,"

"This is personal."

The two ladies returned to their desks just after having stopped for lunch. Buried in the stack of reports sat a pink envelope, faintly perfumed, as if it had been waiting just for them.

Myrna noticed it first.

"Did you put this here?" Her eyes were fixed on Dessa.

"No,"

"I'm going to open it,"

"You can't do that," Dessa said with urgency.

"What if it's booby-trapped or poisoned or something?"

"Maybe you're right," Myrna took the envelope to the lab, where it was analyzed before opening. Inside was a small pin with a note attached, which read:

> Hey, you.
> Thought I'd drop a clue—
> just enough to tease you through.
> *Kisses!*

The pin was silver, its enamel letters (HC) glinting in a purple hue. Myrna recognized it right away as a High School of Commerce pendant. This arrogant son-of-a-bitch was trying to send a message, but she had no idea what that was yet. Based on experience with this killer, the one thing she knew for certain was that nothing was as it seemed. The first thing to do was to check out the enrollment records from the High School of Commerce.

The two detectives decided to split up and follow two separate leads. Myrna would start with 1982 based on the killer's profile; it was thought that the killer would have been a female student there between 1982 and 1986, according to the estimated age. She started by searching archives for each victim while Dessa worked feverishly to track down the scent of the perfume sprayed on the envelope.

The microfiche whirred softly as Myrna flipped through old enrollment records and yearbook photos. Halfway down a page, she stopped.

Libra. His name sat in faded ink beside a grainy school photo, thinner, younger, but unmistakable. A few pages later, she found Vogney, then Crescent, each frozen in time in stiff class pictures and club shots. Only Harry Johnson was missing. No enrollment, no photo, nothing.

She circled the three familiar faces with her pen, a tight ring around each.

"So three of you walked these halls, and the fourth still ended up dead with you."

The High School of Commerce was no longer a dead lead; it was the closest thing to a common denominator they had. And now Johnson was the outlier.

Could it also be the killer's alma mater? Somewhere in

those same yearbooks, Myrna couldn't shake the feeling that another face was watching her back. It would take a lot of footwork to get the information she required. After hours of calls, the answer came back the same. This perfume wasn't sold in stores; it could only be ordered through an Avon sales representative.

Dessa slammed the receiver down, the plastic rattling against the desk.

"That's it? An Avon rep? All that work for some lady with a catalogue?"

Myrna stared at the evidence board until the photos blurred. The case wasn't tightening; it was fraying. Her hand moved almost on its own, dialling a number she knew by heart.

"You only call me when the steaks are done, or the case is a mess," Bob Regnard's voice crackled over the line. Today, he was at the grill again, and she could hear the sizzle and clatter behind him.

"It's a mess," she admitted.

"Then stop chasing your tail," he said.

"Go back to where it started. Every scene, everybody. And ask yourself one question: why *this* victim?"

8

Wrapped in Guilt

Myrna traced her finger over the purple HC pin. High School of Commerce. If the killer had walked those halls, too. Would she really hand them her school like a calling card? Arrogance or misdirection, it reeked of both. Too obvious, too easy, and nothing about this case had ever been easy. Nonetheless, Myrna decided to follow up on the lead, wrapped in guilt, not hers but the killer's, threaded through every taunt and token. Still, determination pulled her forward like a tide. The task felt impossible, like digging for a splinter in a field of straw. Where would she even start? She pulled the UNSUB profile from the board and began slicing the list into categories, grades, teachers, and background, trying to carve chaos into order.

The notes were full of razor-sharp patterns, tight timelines, planned exits, and a signature arrogance threaded through every move. So she zeroed in on the high-achievers, the neat report cards hiding messier truths. Notes from the profiler circled in her mind: hostile mother, rough childhood, paranoia stitched into the seams. The kind of past that left scars you couldn't see. The file hinted she'd gone further, postsecondary. Smart enough to vanish in plain sight. Her notes read like someone who expected the world to orbit her, precise, controlled, and dripping with the kind of ego that demanded centre stage. Somewhere in those dusty cabinets, she imagined a teacher's faint warning, naked and ignored, waiting to be unearthed.

They split the mountain, Dessa dragging A through M, Myrna buried under N through Z. They hunted through the honour-roll kids first, pairing names with teachers, knocking on doors heavy with old memories. Weeks bled away, the list thinning but never enough, hope always dangling just out of reach. Their tempers frayed thread by thread; coffee cups emptied faster, words sharpened, and silence stretched tight between them.

Then came the slip, a teacher remembered Sue. Loud, unyielding, the kind of girl who filled a hallway before she even spoke. A deeper dig dropped the real bomb: Sue was Crescent's cousin. Myrna's pulse jumped. Sue had just leapt from nuisance to prime suspect. Time for round two. When pressed about skipping the funeral, Sue snorted.

"Work, besides, Larry was a drunk and a deadbeat. Owed me more than he ever paid. Why waste a Sunday on him?"

Turns out she'd clocked shifts at the juice plant too, Vogney's turf. Now it was about time and place. If Sue had no alibi, the noose tightened.

She had nothing, no alibi. Not for Libra, not for Johnson, not for Vogney, and not for Crescent. Her breath caught, a quick surge that felt almost like victory brushing past her shoulder. All that remained was the why, the ugliest question of all. For a moment, the case board didn't look impossible, just unfinished.

With the prospect of the Thanksgiving holiday drawing near,

Dessa decided it was the perfect time to catch up with her siblings. The case had chewed up weeks of her life, late nights, cold meals, sleep that never stuck, and she suddenly craved the sound of her sister's laugh more than anything.

She picked up her phone, scrolling through contacts until she found the one name she was looking for. As the call connected, memories of childhood dinners and laughter filled her mind. The warmth of those old memories settled over her like a blanket, muting the metallic aftertaste of the last few weeks. It was a tradition in her family to have buffet-style dinners with turkey, curried goat, and oxtail. This year was her turn. Dessa grinned at the thought of her family tearing into the feast, then winced, imagining the kitchen disaster she'd cause if she tried cooking even one dish herself.

Dessa planned to have the whole thing catered and take full credit for it. Myrna, on the other hand, was busy at the malls. As usual, she had started shopping early because of the excitement felt around this time of year. She knew exactly what she was going to give each person on her list. The first was her little niece, Sarah. She was very easy to buy for, being a doll lover.

Myrna remembered playing more with her brother's toy soldiers and guns than she ever did with dolls. Sarah was her brother's third child. Her perfect brother was also a lawyer and happily married. Myrna considered sending the gifts by UPS, since every comment from her mother felt like another shove toward a life she'd already sidestepped a hundred times.

Somehow, at every family gathering, her mother would find a way to include a blind or not-so-blind date for Myrna. Her stomach knotted. If history repeated, some overconfident stranger would be waiting beside the mashed potatoes. Closing her eyes tightly, she shivered as her brain scanned the last five duds. She could only hope this one wasn't another disaster, though experience told her it was inevitable.

9

Beneath the Wrapper

Myrna opened Pamela Darah's folder. Neat on paper, frayed in life. Porcelain dolls lined shelves in her room; burn marks she never explained. Her dolls smiled in silence, but her file read like a confession wrapped in guilt, each burn a line she never explained, trailing her skin. A secret coiled inside her like a wasp's nest, humming but unseen.

According to her mother, Pamela had been outgoing as a child. Report cards glowed, team photos full of her smile, every teacher's comment upbeat, until sixteen. The entries shifted, withdrawn, shut-in. She stopped seeing friends, locked herself in her room, and collected dolls no one else touched.

Her parents took her to counselling, but she refused to speak. Her father said once,

"It was like she became another child overnight."

Myrna tapped the file, no record of why, no note, only silence where something should have been. She paused for a minute.

Fast-forward: today, Pamela lived alone, obsessively meticulous, her friends made of porcelain and paint. She owned the burns with a strange calm, offering no cause, no context, as if the pain was the only part that made sense to her.

At the hospital, Britney Rellik had a reputation: married men only.

"Low maintenance," she'd once joked, wives did the cooking and cleaning, all she wanted was a warm bed and bills paid. With Elias Vogney, the rules bent. She stopped joking, started waiting.

Her file noted a single mother, a latchkey childhood, raised by a working mom. Colleagues remembered her as sharp-tongued and flirtatious, but friends recalled the shift in her voice when she spoke about him, softer, guarded, like she'd handed him something fragile. The kind of love that waits for a divorce that never comes.

Her record carried scars, too, Johnson's name scrawled in incident reports. A fight, bruises, a breakup. She never pressed charges, but the whispers lingered. She had links to Vogney and Johnson, none to Crescent or Libra, no alibi for any of them.

Scorned woman, bruises in her past; still, motive doesn't prove murder.

Elaine Justif's desk was neat on the surface, chaos underneath. Folders piled, a cracked ultrasound photo tucked away like something she couldn't quite throw out. She held herself like a woman bracing for impact, even while sitting still.

Myrna traced a finger over the ultrasound photo, the empty fiancé line, the dates too close together to be a coincidence. When Elias appeared, she was raw, grieving, and easy to believe. Teachers from her past described her as quiet, diligent. But in her own words, she'd admitted hating Vogney, hating what he'd cost her.

The burn on her wrist remained unexplained. Kitchen, she'd

said. Myrna had written a question mark beside it in the margin.

Even in photographs, she stood inches away from him, like distance had been her only shield. But reason alone wasn't enough.

Sue filled every room she walked into, file notes called her 'loud, dominant, fearless.' Teachers remembered her as the only Black girl in her class, fighting for air, refusing to be small.

'Man nuh look me, me look man,' she once bragged to a friend. It became her life's motto.

She had ties to Libra, Crescent, and even Johnson. Records showed stints in the juice plant with Vogney. No alibis for any of the deaths. Arrests on her sheet, trafficking, nothing close to murder.

In her interviews, she called Crescent
'a loser' and Vogney,
'Just another man with secrets.' But the detectives noted her grin when pressed, the way she dared them to prove it.

Not afraid, never afraid. But maybe, for once, that was the mask she needed most.

Her mother sold weed, but what she really sold was Belinda's safety. File records noted 'domestic risk,' teachers marked her as 'withdrawn, hostile.' Boyfriends came and went, some leaving bruises, some leaving worse.

At sixteen, she left home, couch-to-couch, then the streets. The porn site came later, Suga Plum, camera ready, lipstick glossy, eyes deadened. Vogney, Johnson, Libra, Crescent, all in her schedule, week after week. She told detectives,

'Kept? No. Trapped.'

Her words lingered on the page like truth or performance, impossible to tell which. Her bitterness was loud enough to echo, but bitterness alone didn't tie a knot or rig a car.

High-school cheerleader. College sweetheart. Married four years before the crash. The file was a fracture line: coma, one year, memory loss—ongoing. Divorce papers never filed, affair forgotten.

Doctors wrote she might regain fragments, little by little. Neighbours described Harry as attentive and devoted. Others whispered 'guilt.'

Her wheelchair was never far. But having a motive didn't require legs. Motive required memory. If memory returned, it wouldn't come alone. Natasha Vogney: advertising executive. Married with five children, all boys. No criminal record. File neat, almost sterile. Every answer about her seemed wrapped in soft smiles and half-truths, the kind that left Myrna's pen hovering instead of writing.

- Did she know about the mistresses?
- Did she suspect the children Elias fathered outside her marriage?
- Did she know about the insurance—two-hundred-and-fifty-thousand-dollar policy?

Neighbours described her as 'charming and focused.' One teacher at her kids' school described her as 'always composed.' If Natasha knew the whole story, she hid it well, too well. Her calm had edges, polished and sharp.

Santana Osbourne showed no direct ties on paper, but her name kept circling back in conversation. Crescent had married her sister, which tied Santana to him through family. Through Crescent came Libra and Johnson, and by extension, Vogney wasn't far outside her orbit.

Nothing in her records screamed trouble; she had good grades, solid jobs, no slip-ups, but steady women break too. Neighbours described her as sociable but sharp, the kind of woman who remembered every slight and never let one go.

The connections were faint but threaded, holiday dinners, shared babysitters and birthdays, enough windows to see what others couldn't. Myrna scrawled a note in the margin: 'Sometimes family ties are tighter than rope. Sometimes they choke.'

10

A kiss Among Thorns

It had been a very long day for Myrna. She stopped briefly at the supermarket to collect a few items. She had just picked up her last items from the produce section when a voice behind her dropped the cheesiest pick-up line she'd heard in a decade. She spun, ready to flay the fool with a glare, then froze when their eyes locked, her anger dissolving into silence. Myrna was speechless for the first time in years, her mind grasping for words that refused to come. Her tongue stilled, her gaze snagging on the curve of his lips instead of the retort she'd been about to fire. He was still speaking, but she had no idea what he was saying.

"Come on, Myrna," she spoke low and steady, willing her pulse to settle.

"Get yourself together." Then, through the haze of her flustered thoughts, she heard him say,

"O.K., so it's a date then." Her head snapped up.

"Wait, what? When did I agree to that?" she blurted, but somehow her feet betrayed her, falling into step beside him like a bashful schoolgirl giddy over her first crush.

He introduced himself as Grant, his voice warm and smooth, like a favourite song playing low in the background. They ended up in a cozy coffee shop tucked beside the supermarket, the aroma of roasted beans wrapping around them like a comforting blanket. They talked for hours, about nothing and everything, while outside, the day faded to twilight without either of them noticing.

More than once, she had to clamp down on the reckless thought of inviting him over. Myrna had never been the type for one-night stands, never so much as kissed a man she'd just met, yet there was something dangerously inviting about him. Being near him felt like brushing lips against a rose, soft, intoxicating, and edged with thorns that could draw blood if she wasn't careful.

When they finally parted, their fingers lingered a moment too long as they exchanged numbers. Myrna told herself she'd wait for him to call first, but deep down, she knew that if he didn't, she absolutely would.

There was just something about this guy, an almost magnetic pull Myrna couldn't explain, as if some invisible thread had been strung between them the moment they met. It wasn't just an attraction; it was a sense of familiarity wrapped in mystery, and it lingered long after he walked away. Over coffee with Dessa, she tried to describe it, fumbling for words like a painter searching for the right shade. She admitted she was interested, *very* interested, and then laughed at herself for the way she'd been hovering near the phone, waiting for it to ring like a starry-eyed teenager.

Dessa smirked and teased,

"Maybe it's love at first sight." Myrna snorted.

"Please. I don't believe in that nonsense." But even as she

said it, a flicker of doubt slid beneath her denial, making the joke feel just a touch too close to the truth. Two days crawled by, the minutes dragging like wet laundry. Every time her phone buzzed, her heart gave a ridiculous leap, only to crash when it was just a spam text or her sister reminding her about Sunday dinner. She never admitted it to a soul, but she'd practically handcuffed herself to the phone for those forty-eight hours, carrying it from room to room like an anxious pet owner hovering over a sick cat.

When Grant finally called, his voice was casual, almost lazy, but she could hear a smile hiding there. He explained that he'd wanted to call the same night they met, but didn't want to seem desperate. Myrna chuckled, keeping her desperation neatly tucked behind her teeth. She certainly wasn't about to confess that for two days, she'd been as tethered to that phone as if it were an oxygen tank and he was the air she'd been waiting for.

Two months had slipped by in a warm blur, and things between Grant and Myrna were unfolding like the slow turning of pages in a book she didn't want to end. As she set the table, her hands trembled just enough to betray her: this night meant something. She was finally ready for him to spend the night at her apartment. Wanting everything to be perfect, she'd chosen one of her mother's treasured recipes, the kind that carried the comforting scent of home and love. The rich aroma drifted through the apartment, mingling with the faint sweetness of the candles she'd lit along the counters.

Her kitchen, unlike Dessa's narrow galley, sprawled open and inviting, a space built for wine, laughter, and lingering conversation. A broad island stood at its center, the heart of the room, dressed in gleaming granite she'd saved for years to afford. The surface was as white as fresh cream, threaded with elegant swirls of gray, and cool to the touch. Behind it, a herringbone-patterned backsplash caught the light in subtle shifts, its muted tones echoing the granite's calm sophistication. Together, they created a backdrop that was both modern and warm, the kind of space where wine glasses clinked, and secrets were whispered.

As Myrna set out the plates, she paused, imagining Grant sitting across from her in this very room, laughter spilling over the island, his eyes catching the candlelight. Tonight wasn't just dinner, it was an opening of doors, both to her home and to something far more personal.

This particular evening, Myrna was making chicken Parmesan with stuffed pasta. The smell alone pulled her back to Sunday dinners in her childhood, her mother humming over a simmering pot. She hadn't cooked this meal for a man since her twenties. That alone said enough.

The timer on the stove sounded. Myrna turned the stove off and went into the bathroom. No safety net tonight. Usually, she wore her ugliest underwear as a built-in brake—a trick to cool herself when temptation rose. Not tonight, tonight, she wanted no brakes. All being well, she and Grant would be having breakfast together.

She had chosen a little black dress for the occasion. Her strawberry blond hair fell loose as she removed hair curlers to reveal simple wavy curls. Adorning her little black dress, she opened the door to find Grant dressed in full black. He had on a pink silk shirt that fell over his slacks.

As soon as their eyes met, he stepped forward and squeezed her tightly, gently kissing her lips, his mustache tickling her skin.

"How was your day?" He asked softly, caressing her cheek.

Biting her bottom lip, Myrna stretched out her left arm, pulling him inside, and closing the door.

"You didn't answer my question," Grant said, raising his eyebrow and slanting his head to one side. Myrna knew that the slight gesture was an accusation, as he also pointed out that she didn't like to talk about herself.

"My day was filled with work, and I don't want to talk about that."

"Come sit," she said enticingly.

"So, how was your day?" Myrna asked as she laid the food out on the table.

"Smells good!"

"Now, who is deflecting?" she said with a smile. Grant chuckled slightly.

"Well," he said, leaning back into the comfortable chair.

"I sold a million-dollar house today, so my day was great." Myrna sat down gently.

"That is good news. Is it the one on the Parkway?"

"Sure is." He grinned.

"So glad I finally got rid of that thing." He took a bite of the chicken and seemed surprised.

"What is it?" Myrna asked,

"Are you surprised I can cook?"

"I did not say that."

"You do remember what I do for a living!" she said, leaning her head forward and wrinkling her forehead.

Grant's laugh rumbled low, warm, vibrating between them.

"O.K., you got me. I don't meet many career women who can cook like this. Most of them order out and reheat." Myrna arched a brow, swirling the wine in her glass before answering.

"My mother drilled into me that cooking was the number

one requirement for being a good wife," Grant smirked.

"She's not wrong. I don't know a man who doesn't have that expectation."

Myrna pursed her lips, narrowing her gaze, the corner of her mouth twitching with the comeback she almost let fly. But before she could, Grant cleared his throat and changed the subject, his tone just a shade too quick.

"So… what shall we do after dinner?" Her reply came with a slow, sarcastic nod, as though she'd filed his comment away for later. She rose from the table with deliberate grace and disappeared into the kitchen. A few moments later, she returned with a still-warm apple pie, the buttery scent wrapping around them like a promise. She sliced a generous piece and slid it in front of him, the crust still flaking from the knife.

"I thought we'd stay in tonight," she said, her voice low and teasing.

"Watch a movie… and go to bed early." Grant's eyes flew open, his fork suspended halfway to his mouth. For a moment, his jaw worked soundlessly, a half-formed reply dying before it reached his tongue. 'Don't blow this,' he told himself, heart tapping a little quicker in his chest. Finally, he managed, "Sounds good." Myrna smiled, slow and feline, then slid the fork from her lips with a deliberate sweep of her tongue to catch the last trace of pie filling.

"O.K. then," she murmured, pressing her lips together in quiet satisfaction. Her mind was made up. The decision settled over her like warm water; one look at him and she knew, she wasn't letting him go home.

11

The Family Kiss

Dessa shoved the catering boxes deep into the trash bin, pressing them down with her palm. From the doorway, Deshauna's voice rang out, sharp as ever.

"Funny, I didn't hear pots clanging. You sure you cooked this?" Dessa froze, then turned with a tight smile.

"Not everything has to be noisy, Shauna. Some of us can multitask without banging pans." Darren wandered in, grabbing a piece of bread off the counter.

"You two haven't changed. Different kitchen, same fight." Dianne followed, her teacher tone already loaded.

"Can we sit down and act like adults for once? It's Thanksgiving."

The siblings disagreed about how to handle their mother's situation during an episode. Dessa, Dianne, and Darren agreed it would be best to ease their mother toward the truth rather than hit her with it all at once. On the other hand, Deshauna thought it best to go along with whatever era mom was in at the time. Of course, it was unanimous, three to one. Deshauna won. Today, all the siblings sat around the table playing Scrabble with Mom and waiting for Dad to come home from work.

On the sofa, their mother called out,

"Children, keep your voices down. Your father's coming home soon. He doesn't like a noisy house."

The four siblings went quiet. Darren's smile faltered.

"Mom…" he started, but Deshauna cut him off.

"No. Don't upset her." She moved to their mother's side, smoothing her cardigan.

"You're right, Mom. Dad will be home any minute. Let's play Scrabble while we wait."

Dessa shook her head.

"Shauna, you can't keep doing this—"

"Yes, I can," Deshauna snapped.

"If it keeps her happy, I will."

Dianne sighed, rubbing her temples.

"We voted already. Three to one. And still, Shauna won."

Their mother clapped her hands together.

"Scrabble! Yes, let's play. Your father always cheats."

The siblings exchanged glances, each carrying their own grief, but none of them argued further.

Later, around the dining table, the tension simmered beneath the clink of cutlery.

"This stuffing's… good," Darren said carefully.

"Almost too good."

Deshauna leaned forward, smirking.

"Almost like a caterer made it." Dessa glared.

"Eat your turkey, Shauna." Their mother looked up from her plate.

"Girls, don't fight. Your father will be disappointed when he comes home." Dianne reached across the table, patting her hand.

"It's all right, Mom. He'll be here soon." Marcus, Dianne's husband, slid her water closer and gave her a steady nod.

Darren cleared his throat, trying to redirect.

"So, who remembers the last Thanksgiving we were all together like this?"

"College," Dianne said softly.

"Before Dad..." She trailed off, eyes darting toward their mother.

"Before Dad got that promotion," Deshauna finished quickly, covering the gap. Terrence, Deshauna's husband, offered a small smile.

"He talked about that promotion like it was the Stanley Cup."

Their mother beamed, nodding.

"Yes! He worked so hard for us."

Dessa swallowed hard, pushing her fork through mashed potatoes. Quietly, she sighed,

"Worked himself right into the grave." Even here, surrounded by turkey and laughter, the perfume and the pin tugged at Dessa's mind like an insistent fingertip tapping her shoulder. The notes, the perfume, the pin, they pressed at the edges of her thoughts, like unwelcome guests at the table.

No one answered. The clatter of dishes filled the silence instead. Deshauna sipped her wine and gave Dessa a pointed look.

"So remind me again, why Toronto?"

Dessa shrugged.

"Back then, it felt easier to start over somewhere new. After the breakup, I just... couldn't stay here. Everywhere I went, there were reminders."

Darren leaned forward.

"And Mom followed not long after, right?"

"Yeah," Dessa said quietly.

"She said since we were all grown, she could finally do her own thing. Toronto felt fresh for her, too. But then the forgetting started, little things at first, the stove, directions on her run."

Dianne's voice softened.

"And you were the one who picked up the pieces."

Dessa gave a small, tired smile.

"When she forgot how to get home from the grocery store, I just packed my things and moved in. Didn't even think about it. And when this job came up, I think," she paused, thumb circling the rim of her water glass,

"I needed to be here again. For all of you." Terrence lifted his glass toward Dessa.

"Home's better with you in it."

Across the room, Joshua frowned, arms crossed.

"She doesn't even know me half the time."

"Joshua," Dianne said gently, reaching for his hand.

"Some days she remembers, some days she doesn't. That's the dementia, sweetheart. Not her heart."

"But she used to remember everything about me," Joshua whispered.

"Now she calls me 'the boy'." Terrence cleared a spot beside Joshua and sat.

"She loves you, little man. When the right book falls open, your name is on every page."

The room fell quiet until little Suzy broke in, tugging at Nana's sleeve.

"Come play, Nana!" Deshauna brushed Suzy's curls back.

"In a minute, sweetie."

Marcus rose.

"I'll help Nana up."
Terrence pushed back his chair.
"And I'll set up the dominoes for Suzy. Winner plays me."

12

The Cocoa Code

Now, in the third week of December, Christmas was creeping in, and relief loosened her shoulders every time she passed the Christmas displays, no hosting, frantic prep, nor spotlight on her this year. She still savoured the triumph of Thanksgiving, the perfect turkey, the perfect lie, and Deshauna's fury when no one believed her. Even now, she revelled in the thought that Deshauna tried and failed to prove she hadn't cooked the Thanksgiving turkey and all that came with it.

So many faces, boyfriends and classmates she'd watched slip away because of Shauna. Years she could almost tally like missing beads on a broken string. For once, Deshauna had been right, and no one believed her. The irony tasted sweeter than dessert.

In the back of her mind, Myrna's voice drifted to the easy laughter, the way their conversations lingered long after work. Somewhere between stakeouts and midnight coffees, Myrna had slipped into that space Dessa never let anyone claim. She had begun to feel close to Myrna, more so than she ever did with either of her two sisters. It was the first time Dessa had a partner with whom she spent time outside work. She'd always been very private and withdrawn.

Myrna's teasing voice echoed in her head, nudging her toward the idea she'd dodged for years. It had been quite some time since her last breakup, and she was finally over it. Myrna had mentioned something about a friend of Grant's. Thinking aloud, Dessa couldn't believe she was genuinely considering it. Well, it wasn't as if she had any doubts about Grant; she'd run him through every database she had access to, quietly, efficiently, the Dessa way.

Myrna spent the morning cuddling. Her head softly lay on Grant's chest, as she squeezed her right arm around his waist and slowly fell back asleep. For the first time in years, her body didn't brace for disappointment; it simply rested. Watching him sleep beside her, she finally understood the soft glow her sister always had. Yes, Mom is tickled pink and seems to love Grant more than Myrna does. The trouble is, her mother had already floated the M-word twice, once over lunch and once over voicemail. The lunches no longer bothered her for what they were, but for what they meant. This was real now, dangerously real.

Monday morning crept in before either of them was ready, and by nine o'clock, Dessa and Myrna were back at it. Today's task: sifting through a thick stack of files from the High School of Commerce, chasing a thread that might finally unravel their case.

Myrna sat at her desk, posture rigid, her gaze fixed on the suspect board looming in front of her. The faces stared back at her in mute defiance, connected by strands of red string and scribbled notes. Her eyes drifted over the list of names from the high school, each one a potential liar, a witness, or worse. She was halfway down the column when a sharp voice cut through the quiet.

"Son of a bitch," Dessa hissed, her chair scraping back. Myrna's pulse jumped.

"What now?" Myrna's head whipped around so fast her ponytail brushed her shoulder.

"What is it?" Dessa stood frozen, a single sheet of paper in her hand.

"Another note." The room seemed to tighten around them. Myrna's stomach gave a quick, unpleasant twist.

"What does it say?" she asked, her voice sharper than intended. Dessa unfolded the paper with deliberate care, her eyes scanning the lines before she began to read aloud.

> He screamed far louder than the rest,
> Two kisses given, he earned the best.
> You chase the shadows, Detective Simms,
> blind and stark,
> But I'm the one who sees in the dark.
>
> Kisses!

Dessa didn't smile. She just stared at the note again, lips tight.

"She knows us. This isn't random." Looking at the suspect board once more,

"It's got to be one of these bitches."

"What does she mean screamed louder than the others. Which victim is she referring to here?" The ladies returned to working on the evidence board, focusing on deciphering the cocoa code hidden somewhere in the chaos. They circled the only shared line between them, those three letters: H.S.C.

ATTENDED H.S.C
 Pamela Darah
 Britney Rellik
 Sue
 Santana
 Belinda Ventures
 Elias Vogney
 Larry Crescent
 Charles Libra

Larry, Charles, and Elias had been thick as thieves back in the day, the kind of boys who moved in a pack, their laughter often followed by the groans of classmates they'd just terrorized. But the more Myrna dug, the more she realized their bond had deeper roots than it first appeared. It made sense that life would scatter them after high school; people drift, obligations pile up, and old friendships fade into holiday cards and the occasional bump in at the grocery store. What gnawed at her was how sudden it ended. No blowout fight, no visible fracture, just silence, like someone had cut the string holding them together.

They'd been inseparable right up until their senior year, joined at the hip in every hallway, every cafeteria table, every ill-advised prank. Then, without warning, the connection was severed. No kind of disturbance anyone could recall, no dramatic scene, just three shadows that suddenly stopped walking side by side. By graduation, they were strangers. And no one seemed to know why.

According to the vocational Art teacher, Sandra Daye, right

around the same time, Crescent started coming to class with alcohol on his breath. The situation stuck in her mind because, up until that time, the boys sat together and were very disruptive during classes. One day, it all stopped. They now sat apart from each other and never talked to one another again. No one knew why, but it was up to Dessa and Myrna to find out.

They didn't say it aloud, but both detectives kept circling the same thought: whatever broke that trio in high school hadn't stayed broken. How Johnson factored into the equation was another question that had to be answered.

Pamela Darah was a trendsetter who hung with all the hot girls. Undoubtedly, she was their leader. The group was flirty, mean, and bossy. At the same moment the boys' bond snapped, Pamela retreated into the shadows, her laughter gone, her body changing as if to armour itself.

Teachers called Santana and Belinda the 'artsy kids,' classmates sneered 'rejects.' Either way, they lived on the fringe. Dessa and Myrna felt enthusiastic for the first time since they had caught the case. Now they finally had a strong lead. The lead wasn't from files or witnesses; it was a breadcrumb the killer herself had dropped

13

Sweet Lies

Johnson was born in Chicago, a city with a reputation for grit, yet he carried none of that city's steel, only the soft excuses of a man who dodged every hard thing that crossed his path. At twenty-one, he'd enlisted in the army, but when the reality of service loomed closer, so did his fear. Lacking the courage to face the life he'd signed up for, he devised an escape plan so slick it reeked of calculation.

He wooed and married a young, unsuspecting Canadian woman, spinning her a story about love and building a life together. Behind every 'I love you' was a stamped passport and a path across the border. By moving to Ottawa and pursuing Canadian citizenship, he knew he could slip beyond the army's reach, safe from being called back to duty.

Johnson wasn't just a coward; he wore it like armour and wielded it like a weapon. Every choice was selfish, every bridge scorched the moment he crossed it. He left betrayal in his wake like cigarette butts on a sidewalk. In short, Johnson wasn't only spineless, he was a prick of the highest order.

The current Mrs. Johnson was his second wife. Even after she had been put into a wheelchair, he kept cheating. His cheating was so excessive that he had a whole other life. This is where Stella Monet came in. She was a young opportunist who didn't mind riding Johnson's dick to get what she wanted. Their relationship was, in essence, quid pro quo.

Years ago, when Johnson first came to Ottawa, he met and dated Crescent's wife, Sandra. This was just a few years before she met Crescent. Like a freshly cleaned window, Sandra could see right through his bullshit. Harry's wife had tried for years to get pregnant, only to find out that he'd passed on herpes to her, which often made it very difficult to get pregnant. They had been married about a year before she first began suspecting him of cheating. She ignored the red flags that led to the accident. That very night, Johnson was cuddled up with one of his many women at his second apartment. This, thought Myrna, made him a special kind of asshole.

Friends said his guilt flashed bright and short, gone before the tears even dried. As soon as he realized that she'd completely lost her memory of asking for a divorce, he went back to his whoring life. Harry Johnson was a piece of shit, period. The board in the incident room was starting to look like a twisted dating profile. Four women. Four timelines. One man: Harry Johnson.

Myrna clicked her pen against her teeth, staring at the Ottawa map with two pins blinking like warning lights. One for the apartment he shared with his wife. The other, discovered only weeks ago tied to Stella Monet.

"Why does a married man need a secret apartment?" she asked, not expecting an answer.

Dessa didn't look up.

"For the same reason, he kept changing locks. New girl, new

lie."

"The wife, Anika Johnson, confined to a wheelchair, lost everything. Now, she just sat in that big, echoing apartment, whispering fragments of a life she almost remembered." Myrna was now pacing back and forth.

"Every few months, a new woman moved in. Most women slipped out of his life like shadows; a few vanished so completely it made Myrna's skin crawl. The current one, Stella, was 'just crashing,' Dessa raising her fingers to simulate quotes, but had been there for weeks."

"Before her, it was someone named Keisha." She continued.

"And before that?" Myrna asked,

"Still checking." She continued. "He picked women who needed something," Dessa went on.

"A roof, a promise, an escape."

"And he gave them sweet lies instead," Myrna intoned.

"They found traces of at least six women in that apartment. Hair that had fallen into the drain. Names scratched into the back of a closet door. One photo of a girl smiling, arm hooked around Johnson. Her name was Rina. She died last year. Another overdose, another coincidence?"

Myrna reclined back.

"His wife was going to leave him. That crash wasn't random. And now the man who kept women like furniture ends up dead with a chocolate kiss in his pocket." Dessa nodded.

"At least three of those women had reason to want him gone." Myrna glanced at the board, then back at her partner.

"But only one was close enough to know his every move." Dessa tensed.

"You mean his wife?" Myrna's eyes narrowed.

"Not sure, what if she's faking?"

Head tilted to one side, Dessa agreed.

"Could be possible, except..."

"What?"

"Well, there's the hidden video camera found in his bedroom. The tape found had a few women on it; he was probably blackmailing. That speaks to motive."

"I think these women are stronger suspects than Mrs. Johnson." The board now, crowded with women's faces, their timelines overlapping like broken glass. Myrna leaned back, exhaustion pulling at her, but her eyes snagged on the chocolate kiss taped beside Johnson's photo. She whispered, almost to herself,

"Who hated him enough to make it mean something?"

14

Kisses, Take Two

After much consideration, Dessa agreed to a date with Grant's friend. Myrna had hyped him so high she was sure disappointment was inevitable. Real estate investor, philanthropist, never married, no children. He's either gay or ugly, Dessa thought, smirking at her own skepticism. Still, she bought a little black dress for the occasion, maxing out her credit card on a pair of matching shoes. If nothing else, she'd look stunning while finding out what was wrong with him.

She hung the new dress with care, pinned her hair beneath a purple shower cap, and let the steam wrap around her. Stepping from the shower, she traced circles on the fogged mirror, smiling at the blurred reflection that slowly emerged.

Later, perched on the edge of her bed, she allowed her hands to glide over her long, slender legs, massaging in the pearl-like lotion until her skin gleamed with a delicate glow. The subtle, rose-scented mist of her perfume drifted through the air, mingling with the faint steam still curling from the bathroom. For a fleeting moment, she thought of Elaine's scarred wrist; skin doesn't always shine from lotion.

She surveyed the empire of jars and compacts, colours promising transformation. With careful strokes, she brushed, powdered, and painted, savouring the ritual of becoming the woman she wanted the world to see.

She pinned her hair into a loose, carefree bun, letting a few soft curls tumble freely around her face and neck. In just her black lace bra and panties, Gregory Isaacs filled the room, reggae pulsing like a heartbeat. She moved in front of the mirror, swaying from left to right, letting the music guide her, her body whispering secrets only she could hear.

A smile curved her lips as she slid effortlessly into her little black dress, the fabric hugging her curves like it had been tailored for her alone. She slipped into pink Manolos that clicked against the floor like applause. With one last glance in the mirror, she straightened, a spark of confidence in her eyes. Tonight, she was untouchable.

Something inside her loosened, the tight knot she'd carried for years finally slackening. For once, the familiar weight on her chest didn't feel like armour, it felt like air. Still, she met him at the restaurant, never at her home. Her mother's rule echoed: Find your own ride. Keep exit money. Then, with a grin, another memory: *'Man ah crosses—Men are trouble.'*

She smiled, remembering her mother's vibrance, Warm laughter in her mind collided with the cold truth of the woman who sometimes didn't recognize her. She felt a single tear beginning to manifest. Shaking her head quickly, she took one last look at herself in the mirror, lifting her leg like a lioness on the prowl. Dessa went through the front door, slid into the car, and tossed her head back as though the eyes of the world itself were upon her.

He was already waiting at the bar when she arrived, standing tall with his quiet confidence, quickening her pulse. Rising smoothly, he extended his hand.

"Bartlett Morrison," he said, giving her fingers a gentle squeeze. His grip was firm and warm.

He straightened his cuffs, the gray suit catching low bar light, then guided her toward a corner table. The sleek black turtleneck under his jacket made her smirk. Not gay, not ugly, so what's wrong with him?

He held her chair as she sat, then leaned close, his breath brushing her ear.

"I love your perfume," he whispered. Dessa lowered her gaze, heat touching her cheeks.

"Thanks."

He smiled, the corner of his mouth tilting just enough to make her notice.

"You smell pretty good yourself," she said before he motioned to the waiter. Sliding into the seat across from her, he ordered a bottle of Chateau Margaux as if it were second nature. The waiter poured the deep red wine, which caught the bar lights and cast a rosy glow over their table. Dessa lifted her glass, swirling the liquid before tasting, and then tilted slightly forward.

"So, how long have you known Grant?"

"We've been friends for over ten years." Their words overlapped effortlessly, like two people flicking pebbles across the same pond. Hours slipped by. Dinner was flawless, finished with her favourite chocolate dessert. She clutched her keys in the parking lot like a lifeline; if he'd driven her home, she wasn't sure she'd have made it to the front door alone.

The night ended sweetly, and Bartlett got his kiss. Back home, her phone rang. She smirked, already knowing.

"Hello."

"So..." Myrna's voice crackled with glee.

"So what?" Dessa teased.

"You know what."

Dessa bit her lip. "It went... okay."

"Cut it. Details."

"I'm still figuring out what's wrong with him."

Myrna laughed so loud that Dessa pulled the phone from her ear.

"Well, that's a good sign. If you're looking for flaws, it must've gone well."

"Meaning?" Dessa giggled.

"If you'd spotted one, I wouldn't even need to call."

"You're right. Still... feels too good to be true."

"You're too skeptical," Myrna teased. "Caution's good, but don't turn it into a fortress."

"Easy for you to say. You haven't been burned as I have."

"I'll let you know what he says to Grant, if he says anything."

Myrna hung up and turned to Grant, reading in bed beside her. Without looking up, he said flatly,

"No."

"Please," she begged, batting her eyes.

"See? That's why I'm not looking. Those eyes are not getting me this time." He wagged a finger.

"I just want to know if he likes her."

"Myrna, guys don't talk like that. I'm not calling him."

Pause. A sigh.

"Fine. But not a word from you." He dialled.

"Bartlett. Grant. How's it going?"

"Wait, why are you repeating both our names like that?" Loud laughter.

"So Myrna wants to know about our date."

"Yes, golfing on Sunday sounds great."

"Right there, huh?"

"Indeed, Jack's a pretty good caddy."

"Tell her to ask Dessa." Shaking his head.

"already done that."

"Okay, put her out of her misery, tell her I had a great time, and intend to call her soon. Talk to you later." Grant hung up the phone, smiled and gave a thumbs up, at which point Myrna shot both arms skyward.

"Yes!" But when she turned, the glint of a file on her nightstand caught her eye. Johnson's burned torso stared up from the photo. The thrill of romance dimmed, replaced by the grim reminder that their killer was still out there.

15

Sweet Residue

A search for the emerald green Tercel had taken far longer than either detective liked. With only a partial plate to work from, progress had been slow. But now there was a lead. The vehicle had been reported stolen by a close friend of Britney Rellik's. It could have been a coincidence, but in their line of work, coincidence was rarely innocent. The news led Dessa and Myrna to the West End of Ottawa, to the modest brick townhouse of Summer Greystone, just a few blocks from Rellik's home. The late-afternoon sun was dipping low, bathing the row of houses in a honeyed glow, though the shadows felt cooler here.

Summer was entering her driveway on foot, each hand gripping a child's small backpack. Her two kids trailed beside her, kicking at tufts of dry grass along the walkway. She spotted the detectives waiting and quickened her pace, her brows knitted together.

"Don't tell me you finally found my car," she said, the edge of hope in her voice sounding almost fragile.

"Not quite," Dessa replied evenly.

Summer let out a small huff, rolling her eyes.

"Figures. As you can see," she added with a wry tilt of her chin toward the bus stop at the corner.

"I've been reduced to taking the bus." Her tone sharpened, but the weariness in her shoulders suggested she'd been carrying more than just her children's school bags.

Myrna's gaze drifted past her, noting the overgrown lawn, the peeling paint on the front porch, and further down the street, a rusted-out sedan half-swallowed by weeds. Sidewalk cracks spider-webbed under Summer's feet, grass pushing through like the neighbourhood was raising a quiet white flag.

"Sorry to hear that," Dessa said, stepping forward.

"When exactly was your car stolen?" Summer threw her hands up, palms outward, a deep crease forming between her brows. "Shouldn't that be in the police report I made weeks ago?"

"Ma'am," Myrna began, but the woman cut her off, her voice rising with each word.

"See? I knew reporting it was a waste of time. You cops only care about your own business, not about a lower-class, single, Black mom like me." Her kids shifted uncomfortably beside her, staring at the ground as if used to this speech, while the air between the three women grew taut with unspoken challenge.

"Miss Greystone," Myrna began again,

"Your car was used to run us down one day after it was stolen." Summer now placed her hands firmly on her hips. She looked down, then up again.

"Well, it wasn't me; anyway, you don't look run down to me." Myrna pressed her lips tightly together, her reply clipped at the edges.

"Well, fortunately, we were able to avoid that situation."

Summer, smiling unexpectantly,

"So that means you have my car, you caught the guy, right?" Dessa replied hesitantly, bracing for her reaction.

"Not exactly."

She glared at the detectives, her glare sharp as daggers.

"So let me get this straight,"

"Some thief tries to mow you down in my car, and you just let him walk? What the hell do you even do all day?" The two detectives looked at each other. Dessa shifted her weight, thumb tracing the spine of her notebook, the closest she'd allow herself to rolling her eyes.

Dessa explained that their case was a murder investigation, which had now been connected to her car. She also gave a number for the division that would deal with the theft of the vehicle. This way, Summer could follow up. Further questioning revealed that Summer knew Vogney through Britney, but they were barely acquainted. He hit on her once. She put him in his place, but never told Britney. She went on to say how Britney had been so obsessed with Vogney. She tried talking sense into her, but Britney refused to end the relationship. Dessa wondered why she hadn't just told her about the attempt to get into her pants. 'That sure would have done it for me,' she thought.

Without another word, both detectives turned toward the car, time to dig the dead men back up. Visiting the home of Crescent's parents, they noticed a contrast between Larry's lifestyle and theirs. From the outside, the yard was freshly cut with a flower garden laid nicely at the side of the house. Mrs. Crescent, a plump, gray-haired, mahogany-skinned woman, opened the door. Inside the home was a display of clean curtains and a warm kitchen, with the scent of good home cooking.

The ladies sat down in the living room with Mr. and Mrs. Crescent.

"Sorry for the loss of your son," Dessa began,

"We know this isn't easy, but we've had developments." Mrs. Crescent's voice trembling,

"Please tell us what happened to our son." Detective Watkis, leaning forward, hands folded between her legs,

"We now believe Larry wasn't targeted at random; he was the fourth victim." Mr. Crescent stiffened in his chair.

"You think someone went after my son, but why?"

"We think a woman from his past."

"Can you identify either of these three men?" Dessa showed pictures of Libra, Vogney, and Johnson.

"These three men and your son were involved in something together that may have caused their deaths." Mrs. Crescent, quietly,

"No..." She looked away, trembling slightly. Mr. Crescent lowered his gaze to his hands.

Detective Watkis continued,

"Can you tell us how your son ended up on the streets?"

"Did it have anything to do with his ex-wife?"

"Not at all," answered Mr. Crescent.

"He started drinking his senior year in high school."

"These two boys," he pointed at Libra and Vogney.

"used to come to our house regularly until one day they just stopped."

"Larry, did he ever talk about what happened when he was a teenager to cause the drinking?"

The clock ticked once, twice, painfully loud in the stillness.

"He never talked about it, but we knew something went

wrong; he was never the same after that summer."

"We spent years trying to get him sober, and for a while it worked." He got married and settled down, but when the marriage ended, he went right back into the bottle. Mrs. Crescent sobbed profusely.

"All those years, he drank to forget," Mrs. Crescent whispered, fingers twisting a napkin.

"He wasn't a bad man, just... broken."

Detective Simms reached across, resting her hand gently on Mrs. Crescent's trembling fingers.

"We believe this killer knows what happened. We believe she's taking justice into her own hands."

"Do you have any idea what could have happened that summer?" Mr. Crescent hesitated, gaze fixed on his hands.

At the door, Mr. Crescent stopped them, voice low, almost an afterthought.

"They all went to a cottage that summer. A week away. When he came back... he wasn't the same."

Dessa's eyes snapped to Myrna's; the same spark lit in both. Finally, a thread.

As they stepped into the fading light, they left the family to grieve, a sweet residue of hope mixed with sorrow clinging to the air.

16

Tag, Kiss, Run

With Summer a snapshot in the rear-view mirror, the girls left work together to meet up with Grant and Bartlett. They waited outside a neon-lit laser tag arena at dusk. Dessa and Myrna noticed Grant and Bartlett immediately. They were standing in line chatting. Grant joked nervously,

"I've never played laser tag before." Bartlett continued the banter,

"I can't believe we let you talk us into this."

"Oh, relax, it's laser tag, not actual war." Myrna laughed. Dessa chimed in, her tone laced with a little sarcasm.

"You'll survive... probably." Myrna, continuing the ribbing, said,

"We didn't come to play, we came to dominate."

Dessa raised her arms above her head in a stretch.

"Hope you boys stretched first, no excuses."

"Hope you're not scared of getting beaten by girls." Myrna pointed her fingers as if to fire a gun.

"Don't worry, we'll go easy on you... maybe." Grant shook his head slowly,

"You can joke all you want, but we've been practicing in our minds, and we aim to win at all costs."

Bartlett gave him the side-eye.

"Practicing in our minds? Dude, that's the best you got?" Bartlett, now turning toward the ladies.

"Losers buy burgers."

"You're on." They entered a dimly lit room that glowed with neon blues and purples. Fog swirled around their ankles as adrenaline kicked in. Dessa and Myrna darted between obstacles: plastic barrels, glowing walls, and raised platforms. Hearts racing, Bartlett sprinted down a narrow corridor, shoulder brushing the wall, breathing heavily. Grant crouched behind cover, peeking over just enough to spot a red light flashing in the distance. It was Myrna.

"Got you!" she shouted, tagging a glowing vest from across the room. The vest flashed and vibrated, a hit confirmed.

Dessa zigzagged across the arena, ducked, dived, and rolled behind barricades. Bartlett climbed up a metal ramp, careful not to make a sound, trying to flank the opposing team from above. There was laughter, yelling, the sound of simulated gunfire, 'pew, pew,' and the sharp beeping of vests getting hit.

Dessa and Myrna huddled close, whispered a quick count, then burst from cover, tagging three players in a flash before retreating.

"We like our burgers well done."

Bartlett dropped his weapon in surrender. He shook his head, "We never had a chance, did we?"

The neon lights faded behind them as they spilled out of the laser tag arena, still buzzing with energy.

"I cannot believe we lost so quickly!" Grant groaned, pulling off his sweaty headband.

"You guys cheated, I swear, that last shot didn't count."

"Sure it didn't," said Myrna, smirking as she bumped him with her shoulder.

"Face it, you boys got smoked."

"You didn't just beat us," Bartlett added with a laugh.

"You humiliated us. I saw you crouching behind that wall like a sniper, Dessa. What was that?"

"Strategy," she said sweetly.

"Try it sometime." They all laughed as they walked toward the Burger Pit next door, the scent of grilled meat already in the air.

"Remember, Losers buy!" shouted Dessa, skipping ahead.

"We know the deal," Bartlett said, already reaching for his wallet. Inside the diner, they slid into a booth, still teasing and reliving the best moments of the match. Their burgers arrived, piled high, greasy, and perfect.

"Okay," said Grant, mouth full.

"Rematch next week?"

"Only if you're ready to lose again," Myrna said, raising her milkshake. Cheers and fries clinked in the air.

Dessa caught herself smiling into her milkshake, a soft warmth pooling in her chest before she could stop it. When Bartlett brushed her knee under the table, light and casual, like he wasn't even aware he'd done it, her heart didn't flinch the way it used to. Instead, it opened up. Could it be… or was she only tempting fate, with death always looming?

17

Kisses That Turned Bitter

The Vogney home sat at the end of a quiet suburban street, its once-proud façade sagging under the weight of neglect. The lawn was wild, tufts of crabgrass swallowing the pathway. On the porch, a weatherworn flag hung limply from its pole, the colours washed pale from too many summers in the sun.

Mr. and Mrs. Vogney stood in the doorway when the detectives arrived. They stood with a faint forward slump, shoulders caved inward, as if grief had hollowed them out. His shirt was buttoned wrong at the collar; her cardigan hung loosely over thin shoulders. Neither had the air of someone who had slept well in days.

Detective Simms stepped forward, her voice soft.

"We're sorry for your loss. We know this is hard. We're just trying to understand who might have wanted to hurt your son." Mrs. Vogney's eyes narrowed, not in suspicion, but in something more brittle.

"Who wouldn't want to, after the way he treated people?" she said, her voice sharp enough to sting.

"Maisy!" her husband snapped, turning toward her with

sudden heat.

"Well, it's true," she pressed on, her gaze unwavering.

"We were afraid of him. He was a bully."

Simms glanced at Myrna, who quietly opened her notebook.

"Can you tell us anything about a trip to the cottage back in 1985?" Dessa asked, watching Maisy closely. Maisy shook her head.

"No, that was a long time ago." Her voice sharpened, clipped, each syllable striking like the snap of a match."

"Our son was a womanizing coward. He wronged many women. Any one of them would have wanted to kill him."

Myrna bent in slightly, searching their faces.

"Are you aware that he had children outside his marriage?" Maisy's mouth drew tight, the colour draining from it. She closed her eyes for a long moment, as though bracing against an old, familiar ache. Her lip curled, but her chin quivered, a strange mix of anger and something far more fragile.

"I'm sure there were plenty."

Her eyes filled, and for the first time, her bitterness cracked.

"We tried so hard with that boy." The tears carved pale tracks through the powder on her cheeks, aging her in seconds.

In the strained silence, Mr. Vogney pulled a slip of paper from his pocket, his pen scratching quickly across it. He handed it to Myrna without looking at her. On the page, a name from the past stared up in ink: Pamela Darah.

Detectives showed the pictures of the other victims, then asked the Vogneys if they had ever seen either of them with their son. Only Johnson had been seen once at a barbecue. Maisy didn't think very much of him either. Leaving Vogney's home, the detective knocked on Natasha Vogney's door. It was late afternoon, and Dessa rubbed a hand over her face; Myrna's shoulders sagged under the weight of the day. The front door swung open. Detectives stood facing Vogney's wife, a woman in her mid-thirties. Her eyes were ringed with shadow, darting between the detectives as if expecting a blow.

"Mrs. Vogney, I'm Detective Simms. I was hoping to speak with you about your husband." Natasha placed her hand on her forehead.

"What about him? You already came about his death. What now?" Dessa softened her voice, lowering it as though speaking to a frightened animal.

"I understand this is a hard time. But we've learned a few things... things I think you deserve to know."

Natasha walked toward the interior of the house, gesturing for them to follow.

"If it's about the way he died, I already know it wasn't clean. I heard enough from the whispers at the funeral." Myrna's eyes swept the room, mismatched throw pillows, toys scattered under a side table, and a faint smell of reheated casseroles.

"This isn't about how. It's about who he was to others. Mrs. Vogney... did you know he was seeing other women?"

Natasha stiffened,

"What do you mean by 'seeing'? He worked late, sure, but seeing? Are you saying he cheated?" Dessa, hesitantly,

"Two women have come forward. Both have children. They claim Vogney is the father." Natasha paused, then stuttered.

"Children? No... we already have five. He always said he wanted more, but we couldn't afford it." Dessa placed her hand on Natasha's shoulder.

"I'm sorry, I wish I could say it was a mistake. But they have pictures. One even has his name on the birth certificate."

Natasha backed up slightly and rested her head on the door

frame between her kitchen and living room.

"Did his parents know?" Dessa nodded slowly,

"They suspected. They said he was a bully, not just to others, but also at home. Controlling, did you ever feel that?" Natasha hung her head slightly, then smiled bitterly.

"Only every damn day. He chose what I wore when I went out and who I talked to. But I thought that was marriage. I thought it was love."

Myrna hugged Mrs. Vogney.

"It wasn't your fault, and you're not alone. We're trying to understand who Vogney truly was, and who might've had a reason to hate him enough to kill him?" Natasha held out her hand toward the couch.

"Sit down, I think it's time someone finally heard the truth."

Myrna noticed framed photos of Vogney and the kids lined the mantel. Natasha poured two cups of tea, but didn't offer sugar. Her hands trembled slightly as she sat across from Dessa.

"You said two women. Do they know each other?" Myrna was looking, observing, and wondering. Is she telling the truth? She isn't sure.

"No. As far as we can tell, he kept them separate. One met him at the gym, the other worked at the juice factory where he did." Natasha laughed, sharply and bitterly,

"He always said I was lucky he came straight home. Always made it sound like no one else would put up with me." She paused, and the words hung in the air, heavy enough that no one dared break them.

"Do they love him?"

"One thought she did. The other calls him a mistake." Dessa answered.

"I was going to leave him next month. I had the bags packed in the attic."

"Why didn't you leave sooner?"

"Because he said he'd take the boys. Said no court would believe me. That I was too emotional, too forgetful, he had everyone fooled, you know? Neighbours thought he was charming. At church, he always smiled. But when the door shut, it was like a switch he flipped."

Dessa leaned forward, her tone clipped.

"And his parents? What did they think of him?"

"They never liked me. Thought I was too 'soft' for him. But even they called him a bully behind his back. Myrna, quieter, almost to herself:

"And fear leaves long shadows." Dessa slanted forward, looking at her directly,

"Did he have enemies?" Natasha nodded once, her shoulders slumped at the word, as if it pressed straight down her spine.

"Plenty. Old girlfriends, men at the gym, he lived to shrink people down, to remind them they weren't enough."

Dessa looked at the mantle.

"And yet he smiled in every picture." Natasha closed her eyes for a few seconds, as if to fight back years.

"Because that's what monsters do, Detective. They smile with teeth." The detectives rose, shaking their hands. As they walked toward the front door, Myrna glanced once more at the framed photos, smiling faces trapped behind glass, lies varnished into permanence. The walls felt thinner now, flimsy paper straining to cover truths that tasted bitter as old kisses.

18

Kisses That Lied

Santana Osbourne slouched into the corner of her friend's sofa, knees drawn in, arms loose around herself. From down the hall came the shrieks and giggles of children; life spilling forward, careless and free. She sat so still the cushions barely dipped beneath her, fingers limp against her shins as if even holding herself upright cost effort

The doorbell chimed. A tall, blond woman, polished but guarded, opened the door. She introduced herself as the lady of the house, her voice clipped but polite, and led the detectives through the tidy hallway to where Santana waited.

Dessa and Myrna stepped inside. Myrna gave a small, reassuring nod toward Santana, her tone gentle.

"We know you've been through hell, Santana. We wouldn't be here if it weren't important." Santana shifted her weight, leaning deeper into the couch as if trying to disappear into its cushions. She kept her gaze fixed on a spot on the carpet.

"Go ahead," she said in a low, flat voice.

"Ask what you're gonna ask."

Detective Watkis stepped forward, her boots settling heavily into the carpet, posture firm enough to command the space.

"We're looking at Libra's connections, people who might've wanted him dead. Were Johnson and Vogney friends of his?" Santana gave a slow nod.

"Yeah. They were poisoned together. Always drinking, dragging each other lower. I watched Charles come home with their lies still dripping off him. Johnson promised loyalty, Vogney promised brotherhood; both were just leeches. They didn't have his back; they bled him dry."

Detective Simms eased down onto the sofa beside her, the couch sinking slightly under their combined weight.

"Did they all know each other well?" Santana finally turned her head, meeting their eyes for the first time. Her voice was steady but bitter.

"Too well. They were the kind of men who thought nothing could touch them. We all went to school together, me, Larry, Vogney, and Charles. They were a year ahead of me."

"What about Johnson?" Simms asked, curiosity threading her tone. Santana's lips twitched as if she might laugh, but the sound never came.

"That vulture? They met him at a club in Hull, and from then on, he circled over everything; waiting, watching, picking bones clean." Her shoulders tightened, and her expression hardened, eyes clouding as if replaying something she'd rather forget.

"No one was the same after they met him," her words scraped out, rough and drained, each syllable flattened before it left her mouth.

"Were you and Libra always an item?" Myrna asked. Santana's eyes flickered briefly to the window before returning to the detectives.

"We've been together since ninth grade."

"What can you tell us about Sue?" Myrna popped back slightly, tossing her hair away from her face.

Santana's movement was sharp, protective.

"Don't get me wrong," she said, her gaze steady.

"I know Charles is as much at fault as she is. Sue knew about us. We may not have been married on paper, but he was still my husband." Her lip curled, voice dipping low and sharp as a blade.

"There's a special place in hell for heifers like Sue."

"What about your sister?" Dessa pressed, sharp, unavoidable.

Santana's face cracked for a moment.

"Crescent married her, loved her, then ruined her. And then... she was gone."

Myrna tilted her head, playing her part.

"She died?"

No one moved. Even the children's laughter in the hall seemed to fade as Santana swallowed hard.

"Four years ago. A car accident. She didn't suffer. At least, that's what they told me."

"Crescent wasn't there at the end." Myrna studied her carefully, measuring the weight behind every pause.

"Could this tie back to your sister, someone carrying her anger forward?"

Santana let out a laugh that held no humour, only bitterness.

"If it is, maybe it's justice."

"Do you know who?" Myrna pressed. She didn't blink, didn't flinch, her stare held steady, challenging.

"If I did... I'd thank them."

A long silence. The way Santana's jaw clenched told them

enough: whatever she was saying, she'd lived every word of it, and they were getting closer to the truth. Myrna nodded slowly; the brutality matched the bitterness Santana carried.

"We're almost done, Ms. Osbourne, just two more questions."

"Do you know anything about the doll parts found in your kitchen sink?"

"Look, if someone's trying to send a message, don't drag my kids into this. I clean that sink every day. Whoever put that stuff there wanted me to find it, or wanted *you* to."

"Do you know a Pamela Darah?" Dessa continued. Santana shook her head.

"Doesn't ring a bell. If you'll excuse me, I have to give my kids dinner." As they stepped back into the hall, the laughter hit them like sunlight after a funeral, jarringly out of place.

Somewhere in this mess were kisses that lied: sweet on the surface, but soured by betrayal, waiting to be unwrapped.

Investigation Notes — Interview with Santana Osbourne

Date: [Nov. 2005]

Detectives: Watkis / Simms

Location: Residence of a friend (Santana is temporarily staying here due to a homicide at her apartment.)

Summary:

Santana Osbourne, common-law partner of the decedent (Charles Libra), was interviewed regarding Libra's associates and possible motives.

She appeared emotionally and physically exhausted, but

cooperative. Statements suggest deep resentment toward the decedent's known associates, and a willingness to speak openly about their flaws.

Key Statements:

- On Libra:

    Libra wasn't much to live with. Thought he was untouchable. Always pulling fast ones, always had some story, unfaithful.

- On connections to other victims:

    Johnson and Vogney? Yeah, he knew them. They were all the same — drinking, using, lying. Only called each other when they wanted something.

On Crescent:

- Crescent was married to my sister. Before she died. He wasn't there at the end.

On motive:

- If someone's cleaning house... maybe it's justice. If I knew who, I'd thank them. Cleans sink regularly; knows nothing about dolls in the sink.

Observations:

- Santana holds no affection for Johnson or Vogney.
- Shows no shock at the idea that these deaths may be connected or intentional.
- Considers their deaths possibly deserved, or at least not worth mourning.
- No evidence of direct knowledge of the perpetrator, but she seems to understand the motive behind the killings.

Leads / Next Steps:

- Verify claims about Johnson, Vogney, and Libra's interactions.
- Look into Crescent's marriage records and the circumstances of the wife's death.
- Cross-reference the timeline of the sister's death with potential suspects who might be avenging her or similar women.
- Revisit other witnesses who may have seen Libra, Johnson, or Vogney together recently.

19

Melted Promises

When Anika Bilkard married Harry Johnson, she was promised so much. Harry had cupped her hands, thumb stroking her knuckles like he held her future there.

"I'll take care of you," he'd whispered, steady as a vow. At twenty-five, she'd stood in lace and borrowed pearls beneath the flowering plum tree in her grandmother's backyard, believing every word he whispered into her ear. By the time the petals turned brown and fell, his word had fallen with them. Every plan they'd made seemed to dissolve, first quietly, then all at once.

By their third anniversary, she'd learned to smile when coworkers hesitated before speaking, when phone calls ended the moment she stepped into the room. He drifted through the house like a visitor, offering a grin that never reached his eyes.

Now, five years later and with no children, Anika was pushing a wheelchair into a lonely room, waiting to recover her memory. Harry had shattered every vow, causing her to contract herpes, which prevented her from having children. The irony didn't escape her; she was still defending him, still caught in his orbit, still nursing the wounds he gave her.

Only now, there were others. She had learned about Stella the hard way. The second apartment. The long weekend trips for work. Anika gripped the armrest of her chair. Her hand trembled, but not from fear, not anymore. Detectives Simms and Watkis entered the home. The room carried the weight of stale air mixed with the ghost of faded perfume, like someone still trying to hold on to what had already slipped away.

"We're sorry to bring this up, Anika. We know this is difficult."

Anika answered softly,

"I don't remember that night. I've tried. I only know what people told me, that I was leaving him, but that's not how I felt, not after the accident." Detective Simms sat down beside her.

"What do you mean?" Eyes misty, she said,

"After the accident, I... I forgot the bad parts. I only knew that I loved him. That he was mine."

Myrna pressed carefully.

"Do you believe you would have left him, if not for the accident?"

Anika shook her head, almost childlike.

"I don't know. That life feels like someone else's. The only man I know is the one who brought me flowers after." Detective Simms bent forward to take her hand.

"Do you think someone might have been angry enough at him to want him gone?"

"How would I know? I don't even know what he did to me." She turned her face toward the window, lips trembling as if the words might splinter her if she stayed in the moment too long. The detectives exchanged a look, not because she wouldn't give more, but because there was nothing left in her to give. Whatever truth Anika once held was buried in the accident, locked away where even she couldn't reach it.

Internal Notes from Detectives

- Anika presents as sincere but confused, clearly caught between memory loss and emotional trauma.
- Confirmed that Johnson was abusive, but she doesn't recall it consciously.
- Describes falling for him again post-accident — tragic irony.
- No indication Anika herself had means/motive post-accident; her physical condition limits her involvement.
- Another woman, connected to Johnson's earlier actions, could be responsible.

20

Kisses Between Cases

The rooftop breathed a hush of its own, a thin wind combing the gravel while the city pulsed below, headlights threading the avenues, a red tower winking its patient warning against the dark. Cool air skimmed her skin, cleaner up here, almost rinsed; Dessa thought, stepping from the stairwell onto Bartlett's roof as if onto a quieter layer of sky. She couldn't help the small laugh that escaped; she still had his note folded in her palm, up roof, trust me. Its corners had gone soft from the ride up. At the far corner: a table, two chairs, and a spill of fairy lights braided along the railing, casting honeyed circles like little safe zones, an illusion that the city, with all its noise and teeth, couldn't climb this high.

Bartlett rose the second he saw her, a grin breaking loose.

"Hey." He gathered her in, warm, steady.

"You smell incredible."

"You always say that," she teased against his shoulder.

"And you keep proving me right," he said, not letting go. Her gaze lifted to meet his. For once, her eyes didn't dart to the exits. She didn't mark shadows or measure distance. She just let the moment hold.

The wind toyed with her curls as the wooden table's edge cooled through the thin fabric of her sleeves. She rested against the table and listened to the city's pulse, cars grinding through gears, bass from a club a few blocks away, laughter echoing off alley walls. Yet up here, the rooftop floated above it all, a fragile island where stillness felt borrowed, as though it could collapse at any moment.

"Finally," he said, half-relieved, half-amused.

"You're impossible to pin down, Detective Simms." She tipped him a sly look.

"Slippery is part of the job description." He grinned, pouring her a glass of wine.

He poured, the bottle glug soft in the hush.

"Yeah? You weren't trained to be soft, too?"

"I wasn't trained for anything like this."

She crossed her legs, took the glass, and watched the wine catch starlight.

"You sure this roof won't fold under the weight of your charm?" He laughed.

"It's solid. Sold the building last month. West-facing roof, decent sightlines. I keep the good secrets for people I like." She lifted her glass.

"To insider access." Their rims kissed with a clean chime.

The wine ran dark and slow over her tongue, a velvet echo of the night above. He watched her the way people watch a glass edge, careful, hopeful, bracing.

"You keep me guessing," he said, quieter.

"One second I think you'll bolt, the next you're here, eyes like weather, storm-bright."

"I was built for storms," she said.

"I don't know what to do with Sunny." He brushed her hand with his fingers.

"Let me be the calm after." She didn't move back. Instead, she let her shoulder rest against his, a quiet declaration she couldn't take back. Heat spilled into that contact, small but undeniable, the kind of warmth that made her wonder if saying yes in little ways was more dangerous than any killer lurking in the city below.

"Why are you here, really?" she asked, not quite trusting the softness in her own voice.

He hesitated, rolling the stem of his glass between his fingers before answering.

"Because you're worth the wait," he said, smiling until his dimples showed.

"And because the way you stand over a scene, like the ending's already whispering to you, I keep wondering if I could be the chapter you didn't predict. The one that surprises you."

A breath that might've been a laugh slipped out of her somewhere between amused and undone. She nestled in, brushing her lips against his. It wasn't a hungry kiss; it was slow, thoughtful, one that unfolded like the pages of a novel neither of them wanted to end. When they parted, she kept her forehead to his, breathing the same small square of air. A car door slammed somewhere on the street, and she flinched before she could help it. Her body jerked tighter than the sound deserved, muscles snapping to old orders before her mind caught up.

Bartlett noticed.

"You okay?"

"Yeah," she said, lying gently. The emerald Tercel flashed through her mind, the way its bumper had leapt the curb like an animal. She pushed the image down where the other hard things lived.

He poured a little more wine, patient with her silence.

"You ever stop working?"

She smiled without humour.

"Between sips."

"And tonight?" She lifted her glass instead of her guard, choosing silence over suspicion.

"Tonight I'm... trying." She let the word hang, soft as a promise, fragile as glass.

"For a little while." The fairy lights clicked in the breeze, tiny pendulums. One of the bulbs had a purple tint; it made her think, absurdly, of that enamel HC, how clues could look like ornaments until you touched them and they burned. They sat in the quiet until the bottle showed its shoulders. On another night, she would've checked her phone, re-read a note, chased a shadow. Tonight, she let the case hum at the edge of things, like static you could almost ignore.

"Stay?" he asked, not assuming.

"Yeah," she said, the word left her mouth before she could second-guess it. The city kept moving; they didn't.

21

Portrait of a Killer's Kiss

The morning sun flared across Dessa's windshield, a blade of light so sharp it made her squint, slicing through the hush of a Tuesday street. The glare lingered, blinding her just long enough to make her nerves hum, a reminder that even ordinary mornings could cut. Balancing her travel mug on the roof, she watched the steam drift and unravel into the cool air, a small warmth before whatever the day decided to throw at her. But then, something white snagged her vision, stark against the glass, sharp where it didn't belong. A square of folded paper clung to the wiper blade, its edges trembling faintly in the breeze. Dessa's frown cut deeper, her gut already coiling tight before her hands even moved.

"Watkis!" Her voice cracked the stillness, too loud for the quiet block. Tires whispered behind her as Myrna's cruiser eased up, the slam of the door breaking what peace was left. Myrna's boots ground against the pavement as she approached, her gaze narrowing the moment she caught the tension in Dessa's face.

"What is it?" Dessa only tilted her chin at the windshield, refusing to look away from it. Around them, the street stretched still and deserted, the only sound a far-off lawn mower buzzing like a lazy wasp. No footsteps, no watchers, yet the fine hairs on her arms lifted anyway. She tugged on her gloves, the familiar ritual steadying her hands even as her pulse raced. The paper was cool, almost damp, like it had soaked in the night air. She unfolded it carefully, the creases groaning like they resisted being opened. The handwriting slanted elegantly across the page, too careful to be rushed, too theatrical to be casual. It read:

> *Art speaks truths before the world awakens,*
> *Silent whispers that no one fakes.*
> *Look beyond what eyes can see,*
> *Find the secret left by me.*
> *Kisses mark the path you seek,*
> *In halls where shadows softly speak.*
> *Decode the story, dark and bright,*
> *Reveal the truth hidden in light.*
> *Kisses!*

Dessa read the rhyme twice, clamped her mouth shut, jaw working beneath the strain, before handing it over. Myrna's eyes skimmed, her expression shifting from irritation to something harder, something unsettled. Dessa's mind started its shuffle: exhibits, gallery nights, community events. The words 'halls where shadows softly speak' wouldn't leave her alone, circling her thoughts as if they belonged somewhere she couldn't reach yet. Then she saw it in her head, the neglected flyer tacked to the division board, half-covered by shift schedules. The community arts collective on Cumberland

Street had a rotating gallery. She hadn't paid attention before. She would now.

"Field trip," she said. Myrna got into the vehicle in her dark blue pantsuit and fastened her seat belt.

"Where to?"

"Remember that art gallery flyer on the division bulletin board?" Dessa continued.

"There's a gallery three blocks from the second crime scene," Myrna turned a corner,

"Talk to me, Simms, the killer's an artist now?" Dessa smirked,

"I think the killer likes theatrics. Let's see what's on display."

The gallery wasn't large, its white walls scrubbed to a brightness that felt almost surgical. The quiet pressed against them, thick enough that even their footsteps sounded rude. Myrna froze mid-step. At first, she thought it was just another pastel study, soft and harmless. But then her eyes sharpened, and her throat caught.

"Shit," she whispered. The figure on the canvas knelt in profile, shoulders bowed, mouth stretched in a soundless scream. The shadows curling behind him weren't abstract; they burned like flames, rising in silent judgment, framing the bound man with fire. She waved Dessa over,

"Jesus. That's..."

Myrna finished her sentence,

"Harry Johnson, exactly how we found him." It hit her, whoever painted this had seen Harry long before they ever found his body. She continued.

"But when was it painted, and who's the artist, for that matter?" Dessa's voice thinned.

"But this can't be possible... it was painted two weeks before we found him. Look." She held up the pamphlet.

Pamphlet:
Title — Devotion.
Medium — Pastels on canvas.
Artist — H.C.
No full name. No bio. Just the initials, as if daring them to guess.

Beneath, a quote in slanted print:

> True devotion requires silence.
> Some prayers are answered
> with blood. You were chosen.
> Your sins are counted.
> Your ending is mine.
> Kisses!

Neither woman spoke; the words on the pamphlet had already swallowed the room whole. Myrna whispered,

"It's like the Portrait of a Killer's Kiss, a deadly fate wrapped in passion and pain." Dessa's eyes narrowed as she folded the pamphlet.

Dessa tapped the initials. 'H.C.' She didn't say the word clue, she didn't need to. The date on the pamphlet made Myrna's stomach dip. Someone had painted this two weeks before his body surfaced.

They stepped closer to the canvas and studied every detail. Dessa's voice dropped, heavy with the chill that crept up her arms.

"This isn't art. It's a confession. And she wanted us to see it." Myrna's gaze flicked back to the quote.

"True devotion... silence... answered with blood. She's taunting us, daring us to solve her twisted prayer." A sharp cold slipped across Dessa's spine, though the room was warm. The weight of the killer's presence was palpable even here, beneath the sterile gallery lights.

"We need to find H.C.," Myrna said firmly.

"And fast."

Back in the car, the gallery's sterile air seemed to cling to their lungs. Myrna gripped the pamphlet like it might bite, while Dessa stared out the windshield, certain that someone, somewhere, was still watching.

22

Burnt Kisses

Detective Dessa Simms sat across from her partner, eyes fixed on the crime scene photos of Charles Libra. One particular photo showed a porcelain arm lying at the bottom of the stainless steel sink. The water had long since dried, leaving behind a rust-red outline. The fingers of the tiny doll's hand were delicately sculpted, almost too human. Another fragment, a foot, sat wedged behind the strainer. Burn marks curled their edges black. Myrna's breath slipped out in a drawn-out hush.

"In Libra's sink, Santana swore the dolls weren't hers, or her children's."

"And Pamela Darah collects dolls," Dessa murmured.

"Some of hers were found scorched, melted bodies, missing limbs. We cannot brush it off as a coincidence." Myrna shook her head.

"These aren't just toys. Someone used them to represent something... someone. You don't burn a doll unless you're trying to destroy what it represents." Dessa dropped back, her hands climbing to her temples, massaging with steady, spiralling pressure.

"Or who?"

"You look the way I feel," Myrna said.

They fell silent. The overhead light buzzed, flickering slightly. Dessa gritted her teeth. She didn't want to say it aloud, but the thought was already forming between them. "It's like they practiced on these first," she said softly. "Like the real thing came later."

"Jones," Myrna said as if reading her mind.

"We could call him. Let him look at the doll stuff."

Dessa hesitated, eyes flicking toward the window where darkness pressed against the glass like a palm smudging the pane. Last time we brought him in, he acted like we were the ones on trial. The man's got an ego for days. Watkis's eyes widened.

"So do you. I'm not thinking about him, I'm thinking about the case. The girl with the doll parts, the mimicry of crime scenes before they happen... this is out of our lane. You know it."

Dessa cut her eyes toward her, defiance flickering, but unsaid. She turned back to the photos, staring at the burned images from Pamela Darah's collection.

"Last time he rambled about 'ritualistic messages.' I'd dismissed it as ego."

"Yeah, well... now it sounds like he might've been onto something." Dessa dragged in air and let it spill out,

"He's gonna want an apology."

Watkis chuckled.

"He'll settle for being right." Dessa nodded,

"Call him." Myrna was jolted out of complacency,

"Me?"

"You're better at kissing ass," Dessa said with a smirk.

"Nah. But I am better at pretending I don't remember what I said to him last time."

"Just get him in. If he asks why, tell him the killer left a love note at an art gallery. That should get his attention."

A week later, Simms and Watkis were seated at a cluttered boardroom table, crime scene photos spread out. Jones entered with an exaggerated sense of self-importance:

"You rang." Watkis cleared her throat.

"Don't make us regret it." Jones peeled off his coat with deliberate care.

"Regret comes from waiting too long. You should've called weeks ago."

Simms lifted a shoulder, pretending the jab didn't land.

"We had a lead. We thought..." Jones cut her off.

"You thought wrong."

"The doll parts, the burn marks, the symmetry of the scenes, this isn't just killing; It's communication." He began pinning things on the board, rearranging the timeline, shifting a photo of the latest crime scene beside a gallery pamphlet. He whispered to himself,

"She's been talking to you the whole time. You just didn't know how to listen."

Jones finally turned to face them,

"You think it's rage," he said, "It's not. Look at the patterns. It's memory." The room was silent. Even Simms and Watkis, once skeptical, were leaning in now. Simms levelled her gaze at him, sharp and unflinching.

"Alright, let's start over, show us what we missed." Jones grabbed a red marker and underlined key dates.

"Look at the scorch marks," Jones said. "Someone keeps repeating the same pattern." Watkis's head was slightly slanted, curious.

"What kind of something?" Jones wrote '1985?' on the board.

"A trauma, a memory, it's encoded in the scenes. All the victims (men) of a similar age range were found with some form of oral mutilation or symbolic choking. You have a killer re-enacting something intimate and violent."

Simms tilted her head, her eyes narrowing.

"Like what?"

"Possibly," he said at length, weighing each word like it might spring a trap.

"She, or someone close to her, was attacked. But be careful, she's trained herself to think like a man. She knows your procedures, your blind spots, and she'll use them against you. She wants you chasing shadows while she quietly rewrites her own story."

He crossed the room in three deliberate strides, the floorboards creaking beneath his weight. Stopping at the evidence board, he reached up and tapped the glossy edge of a gallery pamphlet pinned among the crime scene photos. The faint image of a painted face stared back at them, its eyes following the room like a silent witness.

"Now this, this was her flex. Leaving a scene before it happened. That's not ego, that's personal. She's proving she knows every move before you make it." Watkis, taking it all in,

"The gallery note was signed Kisses, same as the others."

Jones nodded briskly,

"Exactly, 'Kisses' is both a signature and a challenge. She's not hiding, she's playing with you." He draped forward, placing his hands on the table, and turned his head to glance at both detectives.

"The killer is in your orbit. That's why she's confident. She watches you. One of you might even know her, but not who she's become."

Jones rose from his chair, the leather groaning under his weight, and crossed to the evidence board. His fingers lingered on a photo of Charles Libra, the first victim, before he pulled a pushpin from his pocket and fixed it beside the scorched doll photograph. The two images, side by side, seemed to whisper to one another across time.

"You need to start asking what happened before the murders," he said, his voice low and steady, carrying the gravity of years unspoken.

"Go back to 1985. Who vanished without a trace? Who was silenced? Who was hurt... and then forgotten?"

He let the questions hang in the stale air, each one heavier than the last. Turning slightly, his gaze hardened.

"Your killer didn't just wake up angry. She's been grieving, planning, braiding rage into ritual. Every step she takes is now seared by the burnt kisses of the past." The room went still. Simms sat with her hands folded tightly in her lap, eyes fixed on the board. Watkis braced back, lips folded inward, her pen stilled mid-tap. Neither spoke; both were caught in the chill of what those words truly meant.

23

The Kiss That Keeps Coming Back

Amidst the clutter of pizza boxes, coffee cups, and scrawled notes, the detectives prowled the cramped division, circling the pinboard like hunters. Photos and timelines overlapped in a tangle of leads and dead ends.

The latest focus: Pamela Darah, the name Vogney's father had nervously scrawled. Simms held the folded note between gloved fingers, her brow furrowed.

"Out of all the names he wrote down, this one. This one we've seen before," she said, her voice low, almost a whisper above the cluttered hum of the office.

Watkis rifled through a battered binder, pages rustling.

"Pamela shows up everywhere, Johnson's emails, Libra's files, even at the Sportsplex before Johnson's body surfaced," Simms said, biting into her sub.

The crunch of lettuce broke the silence like an accusation.

"She went to AA with Crescent. That ties all four victims." Simms added.

Myrna's eyes darted left, then right, eyebrows arching as if the idea punched through her composure.

"And she burns dolls. Libra had charred doll parts in his sink!" Simms wrinkled her nose. She shuddered, the air suddenly too cold against the back of her neck."

"She's like a shadow. Always close, always watching, never in the spotlight." They sank into an uneasy quiet, the cluttered room pressing in around them. The connections hovered in the air like smoke, thick and suffocating, and for the first time, the enormity of the pattern hit them both.

Myrna lowered her head forward, facing down, thumbs pressing into her forehead. Simms continued,

"You think it's her?" Myrna shrugged.

"I don't know, maybe. If it is her, we're in trouble. All the evidence we have is circumstantial. Karamel will have a field day unless we come up with something concrete."

Dessa strode back to the board. The fluorescent lights hummed overhead, a thin line of sound buzzing at the edge of her nerves. She drew a circle around Darah's name in sharp red ink, the marker squeaking slightly against the surface.

"So we dig hard. She's not getting away from this without at least a long conversation."

"Where do you want to start?"

"We need to know more about what his father knows,"

Later, Simms and Watkis positioned themselves outside Mr. Vogney's workplace, the late afternoon sun reflecting off the glass doors. They watched silently as employees trickled out, the street humming with traffic and distant voices. When Mr. Vogney emerged, he spotted them immediately, his hand lifting in a small, hesitant wave.

"What can I do for you, detectives?" he asked. His tone stayed polite, but his shoulders stiffened slightly as he spoke."

Myrna stepped forward, keeping her voice calm but firm.

"Mr. Vogney," she began, her eyes steady on his.

"You wrote Pamela Darah's name on a piece of paper when we last spoke. Can you tell us why?"

Mr. Vogney leaned on his car, his right hand reaching around to scratch his left elbow.

"It was about fifteen years ago, but I remember it like it was yesterday. He'd been drinking and became stinking drunk; he kept muttering something like, '*What we did to that poor girl.*' I pressed him, asked, What girl? And clear as day, he answered, Pamela Darah."

"The next morning, sober, he denied it flat, as if the words had never left his mouth." Mr. Vogney looked the detectives in the eyes earnestly.

"I was there, detectives, there was something in his eyes. He wasn't making it up."

"Thank you, sir," Dessa said, shaking his hand. Both women walked away quietly toward the car.

"What we did to that poor girl..." Dessa's voice drifted, her gaze unfocused on the pavement.

Myrna flipped through her notebook.

"If we work with the timeline of 1985, fifteen years ago would be five years after the incident, whatever that was. Drunks always let the truth leak out; it might be slurred, but it's real." Dessa stopped in the middle of the street.

"But then he denied it. Of course, he did!" A few steps ahead, Myrna turned to face her, tilting her head.

"You thinking what I'm thinking?"

Dessa's answer came sharp, certain.

"Pamela's not just an oddball with porcelain, she's the thread tying this together." Watkis nodded.

"She's the reason behind all of this, or at the very least, the spark that lit the fire." The conversation trailed off as they drew closer to the car. Dessa unlocked the door but didn't open it.

"No, she's the kindling. Someone else struck the match." Myrna paused, cautious,

"You don't want to bring her in again, do you?" Watkis pressed.

"Too fast, we need more," Dessa answered.

"Why not bring her in to talk with us. She might even confirm Elias was involved, hell, maybe others. Who knows how deep it went?"

Dessa looked up and opened the car door. She wouldn't be alone, Karamel! Myrna nodded, and Dessa continued.

"In the meantime, we keep digging." She sat down and tossed Myrna the keys. They drove off.

Later that evening, detectives sat curled around pages of documents, the flickering desk lamp casting long shadows across the table. Sprawled across the desk, records, transcripts, yearbooks, reports, a paper trail scattered through decades. The air in the detective workroom was thick with the smell of stale coffee and the quiet tension of unanswered questions. Watkis's finger followed the counsellor's scrawled notes, hunting for any mention that could tie Pamela Darah to the murders, or shed light on what had really happened in 1985.

Simms flipped through yellowed yearbook pages, searching for a name, a face, a connection they'd overlooked.

"There's got to be something," she muttered, frustration sharp in her voice.

"She keeps showing up in different places, under different names. Always close. Never guilty."

Watkis didn't look up. She was deep in a typed transcript,

a school guidance interview from November 1985. Pamela Darah's name had been mentioned once in the margins: not as a witness, not as a suspect, but as someone to 'keep an eye on.'

"Look at this," she said finally.

"This isn't about what she did now. It's about what happened then." She tapped the page.

"Whatever this is... it started in 1985."

A silence fell between them, heavy. Dessa looked up from her yearbook pages.

"What do you have?" Myrna looked at her hard.

"Are you alright?"

"Sure, maybe a little queasy, probably something I ate."

"You're not pregnant?" Myrna chuckled.

"Girl, please!"

Myrna shuffled the interview pages toward Dessa. She took a look.

"This is filled with questions we can't ask the right people anymore." They kept digging; cross-referencing phone records, searching address logs, and combing through archived therapy notes. Every shred of data was a thread, and they were desperate for one that led somewhere solid.

Watkis slumped back and rubbed her eyes.

"If Darah didn't do this, someone wants us to think she did." Simms stared at the photo board. Pamela's photo was now pinned at the center, no longer a footnote but the name that refused to vanish. The kiss that kept coming back, an echo in the shadows, insistent, unrelenting.

24

The Kiss That Connects Them

A pulsing shimmer flickered above Myrna's desk light. Her office, cluttered with case files, photos, and sticky notes, had become a battlefield of details, some screaming, some whispering. She had gone back over the autopsy report for Larry Crescent, not because she expected something new, but because something had been bothering her. A quiet itch at the back of her mind.

"If Vogney's toenails were in Crescent's stomach, someone put them there. Not ripped out at the scene, collected, hidden, delivered another way." Her spine straightened like she'd been struck by lightning. Her fingers trembled slightly as she shuffled through another file. There, it was the kiss that connected them all, subtle but undeniable, tying the victims and the killer in a twisted dance.

Myrna stood, pacing the room. Her eyes darted to the wall where photos were pinned: Crescent, Johnson, Libra, and Vogney. The bodies, the notes signed Kisses. The stomach contents had rarely been the focus of the earlier murders. She clicked on the recorder instead of reaching for her notebook.

"Larry Crescent's stomach contained human keratin, ground, disguised and consumed. This wasn't an accident; it was sadistic. A message." Someone wanted Crescent to consume Vogney. That makes Crescent a message. Which means...

She clicked it off. Her eyes were fixed on Crescent's photo. Then her voice softened, almost to herself.

"She's not just killing, she's communicating." Suddenly, she grabbed her keys.

"Simms needs to see this now." But just before she walked out, she turned back to the report and added another note:

Find where Crescent ate in the last 48 hours before his death. Who made him food? Somewhere in that trail is our killer...

It wasn't long after asking Simms to meet her at the mission that she arrived. A few minutes later, Dessa pulled up, the tires crunching over gravel. Myrna waved her over, motioning toward the weathered brick building. Once inside, the smell of reheated soup and faint floor cleaner mingled in the air. She quickly explained why they were there: tracing Crescent's meals was the only lead they had. He'd been living on the streets, and this mission was near the Parliament buildings, where he was often seen, and where his body had been discovered.

Myrna had called ahead and knew to ask for Mary, the mission's director. A tall, plump woman with blond hair emerged from the main door, brushing a stray strand behind her ear. Myrna showed her badge.

"I spoke with you earlier about a regular patron," she said, holding up Crescent's photo.

"Do you recognize this man?" Mary's eyes softened.

"Yes... he eats here sometimes, mostly stays on the street.

He takes the lunch boxes we hand out."

"Who delivers these lunches?" Myrna asked, leaning slightly forward. Mary begins to gather containers left by the beds.

"Various volunteers, some are regulars, but honestly, sometimes people just pop in to help. There's no strict schedule."

Myrna pressed her palm against her abdomen. This was going to be tougher than she'd hoped.

"Do you have a list of volunteers?" Mary shook her head, a faint frown forming.

"It hasn't been updated in ages. And with so many impromptu helpers, I doubt it would be much use." Dessa exchanged a glance with Myrna, the tension between them unspoken. Each unrecorded volunteer, each missing detail, felt like a door slammed shut. Crescent's trail wasn't just cold, it was scattered, vanishing through their fingers like air.

Watkis took the list from Mary, but Simms could see that she'd been deflated.

"Hey," she called out, reaching out to touch Myrna's shoulder.

"It was a good lead. Why don't we pull images from the Parliament cameras?" Myrna frowned. "Mark went through them already; nothing turned up." Simms nodded her head,

"I know, but this time he'll be looking for something else." Myrna smiled.

"And that's why I trust you, partner."

25

No Questions, Just Kisses

A quiet cabin on the edge of a lake, dusk falling. The trees swayed gently in the breeze, and the water glimmered with the fading light. Grant parked the car and looked at Myrna with a quiet kind of hope, smiling with great satisfaction. Myrna looked at him, fingers drumming against the dashboard, eyeing the cabin,

"You think you're pretty clever." Grant grinned from ear to ear.

"Not easy to surprise a cop, but I think I pulled it off. Just this one night, you and me, away from everything."

She didn't move at first, just stared at the lake, at the way the trees curled around the clearing. Then she sighed; not annoyed, but tired. The kind of tiredness that settles in your bones.

"You always this thoughtful, or is this a once-in-a-relationship gesture?" Grant, unfazed, replied,

"Only when I'm falling in love."

She glanced at him, but didn't move. Her eyes didn't blink. She felt her palms becoming sweaty. Her lips separated slowly, and she exhaled.

"What did you say?" Before Grant could repeat, she took two steps toward him, a little nervous.

"I think... me too."

He held her close for a long, quiet minute, both of them savouring the fragile, pivotal moment in their relationship. Inside, the cabin was modest but warm: soft blankets draped over a worn couch, flickering candlelight casting shadows across the wooden walls, and a bottle of deep red wine resting on the counter. Every corner seemed deliberately hushed, as if the space itself was conspiring to protect them.

Myrna set her bag down with care, her fingers brushing the smooth wood of the counter. Her gaze drifted around the cabin, cautious, as if she weren't sure she was permitted this kind of peace.

"It's nice," she breathed. Grant's hand found hers, squeezing gently.

"It's ours, just for tonight."

They ate, sipped the wine, and laughed softly, warm, unforced laughter that reminded them both what it felt like to breathe without tension. Later, wrapped in a blanket cocoon, they sat at the edge of the dock. The water below mirrored the night sky, rippling with silver starlight, and the air carried a faint scent of pine and cool earth. Myrna rested her head on his shoulder, exhaling a long, contented sigh.

"Feels like the world isn't chasing me for once." Grant pressed a gentle kiss to her forehead, his breath warm against her hair.

"Then we'll stay here," he whispered,

"until it forgets how."

She fell asleep against him, with no nightmares, no confessions, just peace and warmth and stillness. Myrna woke to the smell of coffee and the rustle of something soft. She was still wrapped in the throw blanket from the night before, curled on the cabin's worn couch. Grant was in the kitchen, barefoot, mug in hand, reading the side of a pancake mix box like it was classified intelligence.

"Good morning, Sleeping Mystery." Myrna sat up, raspy and amused.

"That's what I am now?" "You were talking in your sleep. Something about lasers and chocolate. I figured I shouldn't ask." Myrna smiled faintly,

"Wise." She stood, stretched, walked to the window, and looked at the lake through the glass.

"This feels like someone else's life." Grant brought her a mug.

"Borrowed peace, I cleared it with the universe." She took the mug, their fingers touched, and she didn't let go immediately. "I keep waiting for something to crash through the trees and ruin it." Her eyes lingered on the dark line of pines, where the wind bent branches into shapes that looked too much like figures watching. He led her back to the couch.

"Then don't think about the trees. Just think about now, this moment, me, tragically underqualified to make pancakes." Myrna laughed.

"And yet confident enough to try."

"It's part of my charm."

They ate at the little table with the windows open. The breeze carried pine and stillness; no texts, no headlines, just them. It was the kind of quiet that reset her heartbeat, each second stretching a little longer, daring her to believe she could live at this slower pace. After breakfast, she helped him clean up, not because she had to, but because she wanted to. It was quiet work, soft and easy silence. When he kissed her temple before packing the last plate away, she nestled into it, no tension, no pretending.

"Thanks for stealing me away," she said, kissing him gently. In the back of her mind, she already knew she'd fight harder for this than for any case file.

"Thanks for letting me."

Outside, a crow called once. The day was beginning. They would have to go back, but not yet, not quite. For now, the only kisses were his.

26

Kisses He Tried to Take Back

Myrna and Dessa crossed the street, avoiding a dented Pontiac Sunfire that puttered past them, bass rattling its windows with something that sounded like Hollaback Girl. Across the street, a phone booth stood half-strangled in graffiti, its receiver swinging like a tired arm. A bright red chip truck glowed in contrast to the Blockbuster sign adjacent to it.

The ladies stopped to grab a quick bite; Dessa loomed against the side of the chip truck, her breath twisted in the late-fall air, and the scent of vinegar and cheese clung to her coat. Myrna handed over the cash, crumpled bills and a few loonies. A man in a beige windbreaker lit a cigarette beside a rusty Civic, ignoring the No Smoking sign half-peeled from a nearby light pole.

The poutine arrived steaming, with curds and brown gravy. A reminder that at least one thing hadn't changed. Myrna had just taken a bite of her cheesy fries when her phone rang. Mark beamed with excitement on the other end; he could hardly contain himself.

"We ran recovery on the drive. Found a deleted draft in

Outlook's temp file. The subject line was blank, but it was addressed to Pamela Darah."

Myrna gasped,

"What did it say?" Mark's voice was so happy, you could practically hear him grin through the telephone.

"Wait, there's more. How soon can you get here?" Myrna darted toward the car.

"We're on our way." Dessa followed closely behind. On the way, Myrna filled her in.

"This could be Pamela Darah's final nail in the coffin."

Myrna broke every rule to get back to the division, anticipating the information from Mark, the tech guy. Coming off the elevator, the scent of old file paper ravaged the air. The detectives went straight to Mark's desk, passing by a mirage of technicians busily at work. Mark's grin was visible from across the room.

"Wow, you got here fast."

Dessa probed,

"Tell us what you found." Myrna sat down, and Mark continued.

"I am amazing, if I may say so myself. Johnson used Outlook Express, which stored local files on the hard drive." Dessa folded her lips, knotted her brow, and looked him square in the eye.

"Please speak English."

Mark chuckled,

"Johnson typed an email and deleted it, but I was able to recover it from the file index by scanning the hard drive." Myrna quipped,

"Next time, lead with that." Mark continued.

"This is what he wrote and never sent." Mark pulled the

message up on the computer. Myrna read over his shoulder:

Pamela,

> *I don't expect forgiveness. I don't even expect you to read this. Maybe it's better if you don't. But I can't keep carrying it. I'm sorry for what we did. I'm sorry for standing by, for letting it happen when I could have stopped it. I told myself we were just kids, that we didn't know better, that it was easier to keep quiet. But silence is its own crime, and I have lived with that silence eating at me.Vogney laughed like it was nothing. Crescent pretended it never happened. Libra swore we'd bury it. But I can still hear you, Pamela. I can still see your face.I should've spoken up. I should've protected you. Instead, I looked away, and I've been looking away ever since. That's what I didn't do, and it's worse than what I did.They think sins fade with time. They don't., they sit, they rot, they wait. I'm sorry. I was a coward, and I know that's not enough.*

"He wasn't afraid of her; he was afraid of his own guilt. This wasn't a warning, it was a confession." Myrna stepped back,

"He starts writing, pours his guts out, and then chickens out." Dessa nodded,

"Which tells me this wasn't for her, it was for him, a last attempt to clear his conscience. It also confirms and connects Vogney's guilt."

"Then why delete it?" Mark chimed in.

"Because he didn't want it found, which means he had something to hide. They all did." Myrna sighed.

"It's like those were kisses he tried to take back, words meant to soothe but pulled back in fear and shame."

Myrna shook her head approvingly,
"Something serious enough to get them killed. What about Libra's computer? What did you find there?"

Mark's lack of humility was once again evident.
"This is where my brilliance glows," he said. The detectives ignored his arrogance,
"Go on," they repeated in unison. Ignoring the women, Mark kept on.
"Remember the photo I found originally on Libra's computer." He continued,
"Well, it also came in an email, which he also deleted, but I was able to recover it as well. Unfortunately, the header's been scrubbed; no valid IP address. It could have come from anywhere." Myrna fumed, tapping one foot impatiently,
"Don't tell me you can't trace it." Dessa scoffed, turning the monitor in her direction. On screen, the recovered message appeared:

> *Do You Remember Me?*
> *Some sins don't stay buried.*
> *Some faces don't forget.*
> *You looked away once.*
> *Don't blink twice, I'm coming!*
> *Attachment: pamela_d.jpg*

Dessa looked at the screen,

"It reads like Pamela, and that's another connection."

"No," Myrna retorted,

"It's a planted voice. Not hers." The detectives got up, taking the files Mark had prepared for them. On their way out, Myrna turned back, reminded of Crescent's toenail lead.

"While you're at it, Mark, run those cameras near Parliament again, focus on Crescent. Check if anyone slipped him food or drink. Thanks, Mark, I owe you a beer." She said as they walked away. Mark murmured under his breath after they had gone far enough. "Beer? Who tell you me want beer... ah pussy me want."

27

Kisses of the Past

The corners of the room seem darker than they were. There were no windows and no clock, just a camera mounted high in one corner, its tiny red light blinking in a slow, steady rhythm. One-way glass stretched across the far wall, allowing the officers on the other side to observe every twitch, glance, or nervous habit. No matter who you were, once that door closed, the silence felt accusing.

Sue stepped into the interview room and immediately regretted everything she'd ever done.

"Jesus," she scoffed, eyeing the stained floor tiles as if they might crawl.

"What is this, budget purgatory? No paint, no cushion. Guess misery was on sale."

The cold wasn't just the temperature; it was the vibe. The officer left her alone, shutting the door with a thud. She dropped into the chair, hard plastic digging into her thighs. Bulk order, guaranteed. She thought, cheaper to make people squirm than spring for padding.

The mirror stretched across the wall. Sue wasn't stupid; cops were behind it, watching like it was their favourite reality show. The door creaked, and in walked Detective Watkis, all sharp edges and business. Simms followed, her face unreadable, like she'd been carved from stone.

Sue sat up straighter, her shoulders rigid, but she couldn't resist rolling her eyes.

"Took you long enough. What, you gotta rehearse your lines out there?" Her tone dripped with mockery, every word designed to sting. Myrna didn't bite. She slid the cold metal chair out with a scraping sound that echoed off the concrete walls, then lowered herself into it with deliberate calm. Her expression gave nothing away.

Across the room, Dessa stayed on her feet, arms folded loosely as she pressed against the wall. She watched Sue like a cat watching a cornered bird, silent but present, her gaze sharp enough to cut.

"You know why you're here?" Myrna asked, her voice steady, professional, almost too controlled.

Sue let out a sharp breath through pursed lips, the sound halfway between a sigh and a scoff.

"No, but I'm dying to hear your script." She tossed her braids back with practiced defiance.

"And if this is about Charles, you can save your breath. I didn't kill that lying bastard."

"Interesting choice of words," Simms said. Sue's eyes flickered before she let out a brittle laugh.

"Please. Charles lied like it paid the rent. Lied to Santana, lied to me, hell, he'd lie to God and invoice Him after."

Myrna slouched across the table, her tone flat, every word deliberate. The silence that followed seemed to stretch, heavy in the room. Sue shifted in her chair, her hands knotting together in her lap before she forced them apart again. She squirmed, but her mouth found the retort. Myrna leaned in, voice flat.

"Your name's all over his phone. Calls, texts, fights."

Sue's smirk twitched.

"Yeah, he ghosted me. So I blew up his phone. Big deal, last I checked, bad texting habits aren't capital crimes."

Dessa moved next, slow and steady. She dropped over, one arm planting firmly on the metal table. The steel groaned faintly under her weight, the sound sharp in the quiet room. Her eyes never left Sue's.

"We have you on videotape, bringing food and what looked like liquor in a brown paper bag to Larry."

Sue shrugged, raising her shoulders high and letting them drop again with exaggerated indifference.

"So?" Dessa's voice tightened, the edge unmistakable.

"Larry was poisoned with something he ingested." For the first time, Sue's smirk faltered. Her throat worked once, quick and shallow, before she caught herself and tightened her mouth to silence. She leaned back quickly, eyes widened,

"Bumbo-claat, a dat a gwan! Listen to me, I didn't poison Larry. Larry Crescent owed me money! The man was my cousin, so I felt sorry for him. Seemed like something was holding him down."

Dessa straightened back up. Myrna glanced up at the camera, "What do you mean?" Sue lowered her head, voice smaller for a beat.

"He mentioned a girl once... Kamala, I think? High school days, way back." She caught herself, shoulders stiffening.

"Don't pin that mess on me. I don't know the details, but something happened between them, and that's why he started to drink."

Dessa and Myrna met each other's eyes.

"Do you know when this occurred between Larry and this girl?" asked Myrna.

"I'm not sure, I think it was the last year of high school."

"Are you sure about the name?" Sue shrugs, "Maybe."

"It was a long time ago, and he never brought it up again."

"What about Harry Johnson?" Simms asked in a levelled tone. Sue frowned.

"Yes, your name came up in his records, too." Sue blinked, frown sharp.

"Who—oh, the security guy? Yeah, I met him once. He hit on me. I chose Charles. End of story. Don't make it sound like a soap opera."

Myrna slid a photo across the table.

"Then explain this." Sue looked, her mouth twitched, and her foot started bouncing.

"Where'd you get that?"

Myrna closed in,

"His phone. You two look cozy."

Sue tilted her head, her lips compressed into a disciplined, bloodless seam.

"Fine, one drink ages ago. Charles lost his damn mind about it. Territorial as hell."

"So you were involved with both of them?" Simms asked, scribbling on her notepad.

Sue tossed her hands in the air.

"Involved? Lady, I don't commit to lunch plans. Charles was an idiot with good taste in music. Harry had a nice car, that's it."

Dessa looked right through her.

"Have you ever felt like they used you?"

"Used me?" Sue laughed, short and bitter. She barked louder.

"Used? Please. I got what I wanted. They were the candy store. I just reached for the shelf." Myrna's stare sharpened, mouth opened.

"Then what did you want?" Sue paused; her leg finally stopped bouncing.

"Not this. Not to be sitting in a freezer with two cops breathing down my neck."

A silence stretched. Myrna tapped the table once, slowly.

"Sue, we have three men dead, all connected by something. And you, you keep popping up." Sue leaned back, folding her arms tight.

"Then I guess I'm just the unluckiest bitch in Ottawa, huh?" Myrna didn't smile.

"Or maybe someone keeps putting your name in the middle." Sue smirked again, but her eyes darted.

"Yeah? Then I guess it's time to call my lawyer."

28

Kisses from the Wrong Woman

Elaine Justif sat stiffly, her hands folded on the table, though her posture betrayed a restless energy. Her eyes flicked once toward the door, then down at the blank surface in front of her, mind circling through possible outcomes like a wheel that wouldn't stop turning. The last time she had seen Detectives Simms and Watkis, they had cornered her at work, a disruption she had not forgotten. This time was different. She hadn't chosen this meeting; she'd been summoned and kept waiting far too long in the sterile, humming room.

The door creaked open. The detectives entered with quiet authority, a presence that filled the air before a word was spoken. Dessa was the first to move. She pulled out a chair and lowered herself into it with deliberate control, folding one leg neatly over the other. Her eyes locked onto Elaine's, steady and unblinking.

"I'm going to get right to the point," she said.

"We know you had a relationship with Elias Vogney. You worked together. You had a child with him. What we don't understand is this."

From a folder, she slid a glossy photograph across the table. It spun slightly before coming to rest just inches from Elaine's fingers.

Elaine's eyes dropped to the photo. She didn't reach for it, but the twitch of her fingers betrayed the impact. Her face remained a mask, lips neutral, brows calm, but her hand shifted almost imperceptibly on the tabletop, as though resisting the urge to recoil.

Myrna tilted forward, planting her elbow firmly and pointing with one manicured nail.

"That picture was taken at Libra's DJ event. That's you. That's Vogney. And that..." she tapped the corner of the photograph, the sharp sound echoing in the room,

"Is Harry Johnson."

For a flicker of a second, Elaine's eyes betrayed her. The guarded mask slipped, her gaze darting toward the corner of the image before snapping back. She still didn't touch the photo, but her stare fixed on it as though it were radioactive, something dangerous that might burn her if she picked it up.

Dessa's voice cut through the silence, low and precise.

"So... you want to tell us how all three of them ended up in your orbit?" Elaine swallowed, her throat working against the rising pressure. She finally sagged back, crossing her arms too tightly across her chest, as if the gesture might shield her from the picture lying between them.

Elaine finally spoke, voice low.

"Not all at once."

"No one said you did," Myrna shot back.

"But the fact that you knew them at all puts you in an interesting position." Elaine blinked slowly.

"You think this is on me?" Dessa shrugged.

"We're just trying to understand how four dead men connect back to one woman. Seems like more than a coincidence." Elaine's eyes widened.

"Wait—four?"

"We have images of Larry Crescent in your building," Myrna answered. Elaine exhaled through her nose.

"Harry flirted. Elias was the mistake I kept repeating. Larry? Just the janitor on contract."

"And Charles Libra? There was background noise at that party. I barely spoke to him."

"But you were there," Myrna pressed. "And we've got footage of you leaving minutes after Libra did."

"I left to pick up my daughter. Check it."

"We will," Dessa replied.

"But tell me something, Elaine, do you talk to Britney Rellik?"

Elaine blinked again, slower this time.

"Britney? Why drag her into this?"

"You both had children with Vogney. You both were lied to. And from what we can tell, you were both in the dark, until recently." Elaine didn't answer. Her silence was louder than anything she might have said. Myrna raised her arms.

"We're not accusing you, not yet, but people are dying. We have a paper trail showing that you cut cheques and filed hours for Johnson. Since you had access to employee files, is it possible you saw things you weren't supposed to?"

Elaine finally looked up from the photo. Her voice was defensive.

"Like what? I do payroll, and I file hours. That's it. Harry was a part-time security guard. Charles spun music at events. Larry cleaned floors. End of story." Dessa shook her head.

"Why deny knowing them?" Elaine shrugged, "Didn't remember. Simple as that."

Dessa let out a harsh breath, leaning her head back, and making a slight laugh.

"Bullshit! Not buying it, you're hiding something." Myrna got up from the table and walked toward the door.

"Guess who's in the other room?"

"Maybe Britney will have more to tell us. It's your last chance, Miss Justif." Elaine didn't respond. Myrna nodded her head.

"OK." Both detectives walked out and left her alone.

Britney Rellik sat motionless. Her upper body lay draped across the table, her head resting on folded arms like a child sent to detention, but there was no innocence in the air. Her red curls spilled across her sleeve, hiding her face. Her shoulders rose and fell with shallow, uneven breaths. You could cut the silence in the room with a knife.

The detectives entered the room, noticing Britney, who seemed to be asleep.

"Miss Rellik," Myrna said, nudging her. There was no response. Dessa slammed the door. Britney's head lifted just enough to show the faint glint of her eyes, red, tired, but burning with something deep; not quite sorrow, not quite rage.

Dessa Simms didn't flinch. She remained standing for a moment, then casually took her seat across from Britney. Britney broke the silence.

"So what's this about now? I already told you everything I know about Elias." Myrna opened the folder.

"We're not just here about Elias Vogney anymore." Britney wrinkled her forehead.

"Okay." Dessa pressed forward.

"How well did you know Harry Johnson?" Britney's gaze flickered.

"Harry? The security creep. I met him at the hospital, security badge and all."

"Just met?" Myrna asked, watching her closely.

"How long?" Dessa insisted.

"A couple of months. Then I cut him loose. He kept popping up outside the ER, acting like a stalker. Check my messages, he never took the damn hint."

"Funny," Myrna said.

"We did check his messages and yours. He may not have taken the hint, but you didn't stop replying either. I noticed that you didn't have any pictures of Vogney in your home. Sure, it wasn't more serious between you and Johnson?"

Britney tensed.

"Look, I didn't want to piss him off."

"He got weird fast. I had my daughter to protect. And Elias? I couldn't even look at him by the end."

"Hmm," Myrna uttered, flipping through the file.

"We pulled hospital security footage from last year. You met Larry Crescent during one of his ER visits. Something about a bar fight."

Britney swallowed hard.

"He got a couple stitches, that's it. I was on shift, we talked, and he twisted it into something it wasn't." Dessa rolled her eyes.

"And he wouldn't leave you alone. Right?"

"Damn right. I filed a report because he wouldn't back off."

Myrna flipped another page.

"It says he tried to follow you out to the parking lot, got grabby, and security had to escort him." Britney nodded, mouth tight.

"Okay," Myrna continued.

"So Crescent said some nasty things and made you feel unsafe around him."

"That's true," Britney admitted.

"A year later," Myrna said,

"he's dead, same story, no signs of trauma; quiet death, but not natural." Britney's fingers worried the edge of her sleeve.

"You're telling me he's dead? First I've heard of it." Dessa lounged in.

"You're connected to all four victims, Britney. You had intimate or volatile contact with every one of them."

"And the final victim," Myrna added.

"Charles Libra."

Britney froze for half a second, just long enough for both detectives to notice.

"Charles wasn't just someone you met at a party," Myrna said coolly.

"You supplied him." Britney's eyes narrowed, and her body twitched a little.

"You've gotta be kidding me."

"Painkillers. Antihistamines. Controlled substances. From your floor," Myrna drew closer.

"You had access. He had a market."

"You're outta your mind," Britney said, aggressively denying.

"No, we're looking at your shift records and his sales logs from the burner phone he used for pickups. There's overlap, every time."

"You were splitting the profits," Dessa smiled smugly.

"Or were you just giving it to him to keep him happy?" Britney sank back; her defences seemed to be cracking.

"So what am I now, your dealer, your killer? Give me a break."

Myrna's voice dropped low.

"You slept with Johnson, slept with Vogney, filed a complaint on Crescent and supplied Libra; four men, four bodies." Britney's voice was thin.

"Knowing them isn't the same as killing them."

"But it means you knew every last one of them," Dessa injected.

"And right now, that makes you the most interesting woman in this investigation."

"Well," said Myrna, "unless there's something you want to tell us about your friend Elaine Justif?"

Britney's lips curled into a humourless smile.

"Elaine? Miss High-and-Mighty? She struts around like some grieving widow, but her and Elias? Whole other life, believe me."

"So did you," Dessa pointed out.

"And we have reason to believe you two have been in contact recently." Britney looked away.

"Ran into her. That's all it was."

Myrna inclined.

"Bumped into her, texted her, met for coffee. Which is it?" Silence. Dessa let the silence sit for just a moment too long.

"Four men connected to both of you are dead. One was shot in the mouth, one strangled, another poisoned, and the fourth left to crash and burn. What do you think that looks like?"

Britney's eyes started to glisten, but she blinked them back with a hard sniff.

"Looks to me like somebody wanted payback. But it sure as hell wasn't me."

"Then help us figure out who it was," Myrna said quietly.

"Before someone else gets hurt." Britney rubbed the top of her head, eyes hard, but unsure.

"My head's pounding. I can't take this." Myrna stood up.

"We're not arresting you, not yet, but don't leave town, Britney." As she left the room, Britney mumbled under her breath,

"Biggest mistake of my life, sleeping with any of them." Dessa bowed into the mirror with a sigh.

"Too late for that now."

29

Kisses of Glitter and Ghosts

A stiff breeze blew past Stella Monet, snow slowly beginning to fall as she stood outside the Diamonds Cabaret Club, music leaking through the walls. She pressed against the brick wall, smoking a menthol and eyeing the unmarked detective car parked on the side of the road. She didn't like this, the detectives sniffing around, asking about Johnson again, like it was her fault he went off the rails.

Sure, she'd lived with him in the other apartment. A cramped, dim place where the blinds were always drawn, the kind of space that felt temporary even when he promised it wasn't. Then there was the other place, the one where the locks changed suddenly, and the constant wailing of sirens polluted the air. She remembered the way it kept her up nights, sharp and unnatural, as if the sirens were coming for her. But that didn't make her a murderer. Opportunist? Maybe, survivor? Absolutely, killer? Not even close.

She crushed the cigarette into the ashtray until the filter tore, the ember hissing out in a curl of smoke. Tugging her coat tighter around her shoulders, she let her thoughts drift back.

She had danced for Crescent once, years ago. He'd been drunk then; he was always drunk. His eyes glassy, voice slurred, he stumbled after her toward the dressing room, mumbling something about 'adding her to the list.' The phrase had stuck like a shard in her memory. She'd told security, Crescent had been tossed out on his ass, spitting curses as he went. That was the moment the puzzle began to take shape in her mind, though she hadn't realized the picture it was forming.

Then, last week, the detectives came around. Their questions were careful, too careful. Did she know any other victims? Victims? As if she had something to do with it. She remembered the way her stomach had dropped at that word, how it curled around her like an accusation. Vogney? She hadn't even known the name until she saw his face on the news. Recognition had flickered; he was the one who'd tipped her once, nothing more.

Johnson had introduced him casually, offhand, calling him 'a guy who likes private dances and forgets to wear socks.' Now, all those names and faces swirled together in her mind, a list she never wanted to be a part of.

That didn't make her guilty. That made her unlucky. The car door opened, and Simms and Watkis walked toward her with the kind of quiet authority that made the air shift. Stella eyed them without moving,

"You know, sitting in a car staring at women? Some folks might call that stalking." Detective Simms smiled, smooth and calm,

"We've been called worse." Stella looked from the corner of her eye,

"Yeah, I'll bet. So what's this, then, your good-cop routine?"

"Just a conversation," Myrna answered.

She popped her gum against her teeth.

"Unless you're buying, you're wasting my break." Myrna cleared her throat,

"We're looking into someone you might've known, Charles Libra. A flicker crossed Stella's face, not fear, something colder, recognition. A slight beat passed.

"A lot of guys come through here, can't say I remember all their names." Myrna took two steps toward her,

"We think you remember this one," Stella smirks and lights another cigarette,

"Think all you want, that doesn't make it true."

Simms stood shoulder to shoulder with Myrna, her hands tucked in her coat pockets as her eyes fixed on the woman across from them.

"We heard you had history," she said evenly.

"That he used to stop by here and ask for you, is that true?" Stella took a slow drag from her cigarette, the tip glowing red in the dim light. Smoke curled from her lips as she smirked.

"What are you building, a scrapbook or something?" Her voice carried a rasp, weary and edged with disdain.

"Just trying to understand the nature of your relationship," Myrna replied, her tone measured, professional. Stella exhaled through her nose, sending a ribbon of smoke into the night.

"Simple enough. He paid, he watched, he left. Same as a hundred others, nothing special." Simms tilted her head, studying Stella through the haze of smoke. Her gaze was sharp, unblinking.

"Except he's dead now," she said firmly.

"And you changed your number the day after."

The words landed. Stella tapped her cigarette against the wall, flakes of ash scattering. Her eyes shifted, the easy defiance dimming, replaced by something quick, something calculating.

"Maybe I was tired of shadows following me. Or maybe I just don't answer calls from ghosts."

Simms gave a short, dry chuckle.

"You think he was a ghost?" Stella wrestled against the wall, smoke drifting lazily from her fingers as she gave a thin, knowing smile.

"No. But I think whatever he was hiding, someone didn't like it." Myrna's brows lifted slightly as she tightened the space between them, curiosity sharpening her features.

"And that someone wasn't you?" Stella's eyes cut toward her, steady now, the hint of a challenge glinting in them. She stubbed out the cigarette with deliberate slowness, grinding it flat.

"If I wanted him gone, he'd have been gone a long time ago. Now, unless you got cash or a check, I've got music to dance to." She turned and walked back inside, leaving a curl of smoke and silence behind her.

Belinda Ventures adjusted her webcam, carefully blurring the background. She'd cleaned up since the call from the detectives. She hid the fan gifts, the unopened chocolate kisses, and the lingerie from her wish list. They'd asked about Vogney. She said she didn't know him personally, just a screen name. That was true, technically.

Vogney had been a regular, quiet, but specific. He asked for odd things, not sex, just little performances. Read a poem, wear gloves, cry a little on the knees. He was more than a little bossy. She thought he might be a writer or something. Johnson had been different, loud, flashy and demanding. He tipped big and vanished for weeks. She figured he was rich or high or both. Libra... Libra scared her. He hadn't said much, but he stared. It was like he could see her off-camera.

And Crescent? That name rang a bell. Wasn't he the one who messaged her in the middle of the night once, misspelling every word? He called himself 'a friend of the floor crew.' Something about 'cleaning up after the sins of men.' She blocked him, then got another message. New account, she told herself, it was just trolls, lonely men who were harmless.

The small café was nearly empty. A single espresso machine hissed in the background while rain tapped rhythmically on the windows. Belinda Ventures sat across from the two detectives, sunglasses pushed into her sleek hair. She stirred her tea slowly, refusing to meet either of their eyes. Myrna Watkis opened the folder in front of her.

"You went to the High School of Commerce, graduated in 1987, is that right?" Belinda's hand paused.

"Oh, so graduating's a crime now?"

"Not at all," Dessa replied, her tone mild.

"We just found it interesting. You're one of eight people on our list who went there, and you're connected, in one way or another, to all four victims."

Belinda exhaled through her nose.

"That school was a dump. Half didn't make it out, and the rest of us probably wish we hadn't."

"You know a Pamela Darah?" Myrna asked casually. Belinda looked up sharply.

"Yeah, she was… around, head cheerleader. She ran with Britney and Greg Stone. Greg was sweet. Pamela and Britney? They thought they were royalty. They called themselves the Honeycomb."

That got both detectives' attention. Myrna bent forward.

"What about Charles Libra?" Belinda gave a dry laugh.

"Libra? Two grades up. Always hung around after school in his car. That alone should tell you everything."

"Who is this Greg Stone?" Belinda shook her head,

"He died in the early nineties. AIDS."

Dessa flipped a page.

"And Crescent, you recognize the name?" Belinda hesitated.

"He was odd. Always scribbling in that notebook, reeking of rum and cigarettes. I think he dropped out." People laughed at him behind his back.

"And Vogney?" She made a face. "I don't remember much. He played football. He was one of the golden boys. They all were, weren't they?

"Funny thing? Not one of them remembered me from high school. Not one."

A long silence stretched between them. Finally, Myrna slid a photo across the table, the silver pin, HC in block letters.

"The killer left us this, along with a note. We think it all started there." Belinda's lips tightened.

"Then maybe you should be asking the ones who lit the fire in the first place."

Dessa tilted her head.

"Started what?" Belinda stared into her tea.

"You ever been to a party and realized everyone was laughing at a joke you didn't get… and then you realize you're the punchline?" Myrna spoke carefully.

"Something happened in 1985." Belinda didn't move.

"A lot happened in 1985."

"You were fifteen," Dessa said quietly.

"So were a lot of girls."

A crack formed in her tone, but she masked it quickly. She stood, gathering her bag.

"You dig up high school ghosts, you'll find more bones than you can carry. And under those bones? Just glitter and gold, and fake as hell." She left the tea untouched.

30

Kisses from Honeycomb

The squad room was quiet, save for the clack of Myrna's pen against the edge of her notebook. She stood at the evidence board, hands in her pockets, eyes growing weary.

"Let's look at the board again," she said flatly,

"top to bottom." Dessa huddled against the table behind her, coffee in hand, legs crossed.

"All right." Myrna pointed to the board.

"Victim one: Charles Libra, DJ, dealer. Killed in his apartment, bacon grease, strangled, locks cut, and chocolate kisses left in the bathroom vase. Johnson's penis was in his mouth. Lying in blood, not his own. Doll parts in the sink. No forced entry."

"Victim two," Dessa continued, "Harry Johnson. Shot in the mouth. Bound, burned, and posed on his knees in a storage closet at the sports complex. A bag of chocolate kisses was in his jacket. Forensics confirmed blood loss, embalming fluid, and a six-week-old time of death. He was already dead before the fire."

"Victim three: Elias Vogney," Myrna said, moving to the

next photo.

"Van crashed at Rockcliffe Lookout. Pepper spray in the vents and the brake line cut. Bottles of juice were found at the scene. Died from a heart attack mid-crash. Pictures of women were scattered nearby, and more chocolate kisses were found embedded inside a manual in the dash."

"Victim four," Dessa said softly, "Larry Crescent. Found near Parliament. Presumed drunk, actually poisoned. Arsenic and ground-up toenails in his stomach. A crude sketch of a smiling jackass was drawn on his back. Kisses and note found in discarded paper bag."

They were quiet for a moment. Four men, four bodies, four scenes dressed in cruelty, symbolism, and just enough misdirection to keep them chasing shadows. Myrna grabbed the dry-erase marker and wrote across the top:

ALL VICTIMS: MALE, BLACK, CONNECTED TO WOMEN UNDER INVESTIGATION.

"Suspects," she said, pointing.

"Britney Rellik," Dessa listed.

"Nurse, had a child with Vogney. Flirted with Johnson, treated Crescent, and supplied Libra with stolen meds."

"Elaine Justif, secretary, also had a child with Vogney. Appeared in the background of multiple photos with victims. Keeps things polished and tight, too tight."

"Stella Monet," Myrna added,

"Lived with Johnson and had an encounter with Crescent. Worked at the club where Libra frequented. Something happened between them that wasn't reported."

"Belinda Ventures," Dessa said, "an online adult performer, says she only interacted with Crescent once, but we know she worked in places Libra and Johnson both frequented. Might've seen something, might've been used."

"And Pamela Darah," Myrna said last,

"The wildcard, her name shows up on two computers with e-mails and a photo. She calls herself an artist obsessed with faces. Then shows up at Libra's funeral just to see his face in a box." They stood looking at the board again, piercingly.

"And now we know about Larry's book," Myrna turned to face Dessa. "We've got to find that book."

"Belinda said he carried it everywhere," Dessa added,

"Wrote in it constantly." Myrna flipped through her notebook,

"Honeycomb, that's what Elaine and Pamela called themselves."

"H.C.," Dessa added. Myrna circled it with her pen.

"It's the same way the artist signed the painting."

"You think it's them, working together?" Dessa asked in a neutral tone.

"I think this more than implicates them," Myrna said.

"And it just became the most important thing on this board."

The detectives left the division to investigate and delve further into Crescent's background. Myrna and Dessa decided to speak to social workers, shelter workers, and acquaintances. They went back to the shelter where he was known to frequent. It was confirmed that Larry wasn't just a drunk; he kept notes, watched people, and wrote things down. He may have known more about the other victims than he let on.

Nothing was found in the stuff he left behind at the shelter. One of the ladies at the shelter remembered he said something about being watched by the queen bee. They decided to speak to the other homeless people who hung out where he slept. One man, known as Spoons, sat hunched beneath a heat grate, rolling a cigarette with fingers stained dark from dirt and rain. He recognized Larry's name immediately.

"Crazy old bastard, but sharp. Always muttering into some busted recorder, scribbling in that notebook he never let anyone touch."

"What kind of things did he talk about?" Myrna asked, her voice calm, deliberate, as if coaxing a child to recall a dream. Spoons shrugged, the motion slow and careless, like his shoulders were too heavy for his frame.

"Women, men, bad things. Sometimes he'd say, *She's not done yet.*" His eyes flicked to the floor, then back up.

"I figured he meant some woman from his past, maybe a daughter, maybe a ghost."

Dessa shifted her weight, drawing back slightly, one hand pressed to her nose. The sour mix of sweat and stale smoke rolling off Spoons made her eyes water, but she kept her tone even.

"Did he ever say names?" He hesitated, lips pulling tight over yellowed teeth.

"Vogney, for sure. He said that name when he was pissed, and Johnson once. He said he owed him something and called him a coward." A short, bitter laugh rattled from his throat.

"Larry had enemies, but he wasn't scared of 'em."

"Did he ever mention anyone named Pamela?" Myrna pressed, pencil poised above her notebook. Spoons staggered back, scratching the wiry scruff at his jaw, thinking it over. A long silence stretched before he finally spoke.

"No, but he talked about *the honey lady.* Said she had sugar eyes and a knife for a tongue."

"He called her 'H.C.' once." He tapped a finger against the side of his cardboard box as if the memory had just resurfaced.

"Now that you say it, I thought it was some code, like he was waiting for her to come back."

Myrna's pencil moved quickly, her eyes narrowing in thought.

"If he said H.C. and referred to a woman, that connects to Honeycomb." She glanced at Dessa, then back to Spoons.

"And if Pamela and Britney were tracking these guys... it could be he knew they were all in danger before anyone else did."

They handed Spoons a few dollars and a business card.

"If you remember anything else, call us, day or night," Dessa said. Spoons nodded, then tapped the side of his head.

"Larry said one more thing, too, right before he disappeared for a while. He said: They all wore masks, but I saw their real faces." Myrna turned back toward the car. The pieces weren't falling into place yet, but they were starting to hum in tune.

31

Kisses Between the Lines

Dessa woke with a jolt, her hand flying to her neck. A hot, searing pain burned deep into the left side, radiating down toward her shoulder. She grimaced, trying to turn her head, but the stiff pull made her wince. A pinched nerve, maybe. She massaged the sore spot with slow, tentative circles, feeling the knot of tension pressing back against her fingers.

Carefully, she swung her legs over the side of the bed and eased herself upright. The apartment was still cloaked in morning quiet, the faint hum of the refrigerator the only sound as she padded barefoot across the hallway. She nudged her mother's door open. Her mother lay curled beneath the quilt, a faint wheeze threading through her steady breaths. The sight eased something in Dessa's chest. She bent down, gently tucking the blanket under her mother's chin, smoothing a loose strand of hair away from her temple. For a moment, Dessa lingered, listening to the fragile rhythm of sleep, then tiptoed out, closing the door with practiced silence.

The new routine they'd pieced together with her siblings felt both comforting and heavy, like an unspoken contract they all carried. Diane covered the days when Dessa worked late or was called out unexpectedly; it wasn't perfect, but it kept their mother cared for. Dessa busied herself in the kitchen, whisking eggs and setting bread into the toaster, moving slowly while the stiffness in her neck reminded her of every turn. She ate without much appetite, got dressed, and waited by the window for Diane's knock. When her sister arrived, they exchanged a brief but warm goodbye, that quick squeeze of hands that had become their silent reassurance.

Stepping out into the cool morning air, Dessa drew in a long breath. The sky was pale, streaked with early sunlight, and the city was already stirring awake. Her mind, though, wasn't on the day's small comforts. It was racing ahead, restless, focused on a single thread she couldn't shake. Today, she would find that damn book. While Myrna checked in with the forensics lab, Dessa trusted her instincts. Something told her that if Larry had hidden anything, it would be tucked away in the familiar shadows of his parents' home.

The lab doors groaned as Myrna pushed them open, the weighted metal giving way with reluctant force. Inside, the air was sharp with disinfectant, tinged with the faint copper of chemicals. Rows of fluorescent lights buzzed overhead, their glow bleaching the room into stark whites and grays. Technicians bent over microscopes and glowing monitors, their movements precise and almost mechanical, the faint scratching of pens and the soft click of keyboards layering into a steady, clinical rhythm.

"Any new developments on my serial killer case?" Myrna's voice cut across the room, tight and urgent, demanding attention. A technician, his sleeves rolled to his elbow, sifted through a stack of evidence bags. He looked up only briefly, the powder on his gloves smeared across the plastic.

"We pulled a partial print inside the doll's head from Libra's sink," he said. His voice was flat, matter-of-fact.

"Clean, but nothing in the database yet."

Myrna stepped closer, the heels of her shoes echoing sharply against the linoleum.

"Anything else?" The man hesitated, then turned to a monitor, scrolling quickly. His shoulders sagged as he shook his head.

"Were you able to find a book in Crescent's belongings?" she asked, her tone laced with restrained urgency.

"We've got two guys out," he answered, avoiding her eyes.

"We're behind. There were three books found, but we haven't been able to crack the code."

Her jaw dropped, fury rising hot in her chest.

"Why wasn't I informed?" The technician shifted under her stare, throat bobbing.

"I don't know. I filed the report three months ago." Myrna drew in a slow breath through her nose, forcing her pulse to settle.

"Let me see the books."

He led her down a narrow aisle to a back table. Three slim notebooks sat side by side, their covers flaking, edges curled, spines brittle from years of handling. The pages inside were swollen and warped as though they had been left in damp air too long, smelling faintly of mildew and ink.

Myrna slipped on a pair of gloves and opened the first one. Jagged handwriting crawled across the pages in erratic patterns, letters slanted and tangled, as though written in haste or madness. One word surfaced over and over, scrawled with almost ritualistic obsession: Honeycomb.

She flipped to another page and froze. A rough sketch, two crude stick figures labelled B and P, was circled several times, the ring surrounded by uneven doodles of kisses. The childishness of the drawing only made it more unsettling, like something torn from the margins of a disturbed child's notebook. The weight of it pressed down on her chest. This wasn't just a journal; it was a map into a fractured mind.

Myrna took out her phone and photographed as many pages as she could.

"I need these results as soon as possible." She headed to the division. Meanwhile, in the dim garage of Crescent's childhood home, Dessa wiped sweat from her brow and shoved another dusty box aside. She'd been at it for over an hour, going through old newspapers, broken VHS tapes, and bits of junk that hadn't mattered to anyone in decades.

Ready to give up, she paused and scanned the room one more time. Then she saw it, tucked into the darkest corner, behind an old coat rack, a box warped at the edges labelled 'High School' in thick black marker.

"Jackpot," she said aloud.

She opened the box. It was filled with a school sweater with moth holes. A cheerleading button labelled Honeycomb, a cassette mix tape labelled 'For H.C.' with handwritten playlist tracks like Karma Chameleon and Every Breath You Take. There was a yearbook from the High School of Commerce with a photo of Britney and Pamela at the front of the squad, signed Honeycomb forever. Another book was found inside the box, wrapped in plastic and bound with a shoelace: a small red journal, the cover labelled, *Summer, 1985.*

Simms knew she had Larry's book. She sat on a crate and opened it carefully, and nothing was legible to the naked eye except

"Honeycomb ruined everything. Don't forget." Everything else was written in code. Dessa stared at it for a long moment. She had Larry's book. She stood, gathered the contents, and carefully packed them into the box. As she drove back to the division, her mind buzzed with questions, possibilities, and the one truth she couldn't ignore: Pamela and Britney weren't just linked to the victims. They were the thread that tied them all together.

The squad room hummed with low conversation and the click of keyboards. Myrna entered briskly, a folder tucked under her arm. Dessa was already there, dropping a cardboard box onto her desk. Myrna eyed the box,

"Tell me that's what I think it is." Dessa smiled, "If you think it's Larry Crescent's brain on paper, then yeah, I think I found it."

"You went through the parents' place?" "Garage, buried under thirty years of junk. The box was marked High School. I found a cheerleading button that says Honeycomb, a yearbook, and this." She pulled out the journal and handed it over. Dessa continued,

"Diary, from his summer '85. Most of it is coded, but look at the first line." Myrna read aloud,

"Honeycomb ruined everything. Don't forget." She looked up.

"Jesus!" Dessa passed her the yearbook.

"Pamela and Britney were Honeycomb. The yearbook photo confirmed it, front row and center."

"I just came from the lab," said Myrna,

"They've had three notebooks from Crescent in evidence for months, but didn't bother to tell me. One of them is filled with drawings. Stick figures labelled B and P. Surrounded by kisses." Dessa's eyes widened,

"It's not subtle anymore, is it?"

"No, and it's not just obsession; he was documenting something, tracking people, watching."

"He knew Libra, Johnson, and Vogney, and he either saw or was involved with what happened to someone back then."

Silence for a moment, Myrna, massaged her temples.

"The thing is... I'm not sure if Pamela and Britney were the abusers or the abused, or both." Dessa tilted her head.

"My money is on both. Larry was more than a victim. That's why his notes are such a mess; he wasn't just paranoid, he was haunted." Myrna rose quietly.

"And now we're all one step behind someone who might be crossing names off an old list. Time to figure out who was there that summer. Who hurt whom, and who's killing for it now?" Dessa picked up the book,

"I'll start decoding this journal. Maybe he left us a map, or a confession."

"And I'll ask for a meeting to review the ITO and get a warrant. It's time we talk to Pamela Darah again, with pressure."

32

Bittersweet Trails

"You're telling me we don't have enough?" Myrna moved toward the desk, palms flat, voice even, too even. The Crown attorney didn't blink.

"Not for a warrant, not for Darah. Suspicion, yes, trauma, sure. But without hard evidence? It'll get tossed before it hits a judge's desk."

"We have her on surveillance entering the building where Johnson was found dead."

"And she's an artist, artists wander, artists observe, artists get misread. You want a warrant, you need more than movement and metaphor."

Dessa sat back, swirling her coffee like it held the answer. Myrna could feel the tension vibrating in her partner's shoulders.

"So let me get this straight,"

"You want us to wait until she leaves a kiss on someone else's body, then we have something real?"

"I'm saying," the attorney replied,

"You have pieces, not a picture." The conversation ended

with a clipped nod. Compared to the outside air, the division air felt heavier. Myrna's fingers trembled slightly.

"You all right?" Dessa asked.

"No, but let's pretend I am."

They walked toward the evidence board in silence. Myrna stared at the scrawl of notes from Crescent's coded journal, still pinned in translation.

"He wrote about a place where the paint bled. Tuesdays, twins still buzz. B and P."

"You thinking what I'm thinking?" Dessa nodded.

"Yeah. Let's find the wall." They parked off a side road behind the abandoned rail line near Alta Vista, a stretch of cracked pavement and chain-link fences, where old graffiti still clung to crumbling concrete. This was the kind of place teenagers went to feel invisible. A place for secrets, dares, and first betrayals. Myrna stood still for a moment, eyes scanning the underpass walls, and then she saw it.

"There," she said, pointing to a faded mural, barely visible under layers of new tags and grime. But in the center, almost lovingly preserved, was a signature in pink paint: H.C. A heart drawn around it. A jagged crack scratched through the middle.

"Honeycomb," Dessa whispered. Myrna crouched near the wall, brushing dirt off with her sleeve. Nothing but old tags and grime. She rocked back on her heels, frustration creeping in. Then, just as she turned, something caught the light, a thin glint of metal peeking from behind a rusted drainage pipe. She reached in and tugged free an old, dented, dirty cookie tin, sealed shut with dried tape.

Inside were fragments: a broken doll arm, a melted chocolate kiss still half-wrapped in foil, and a blurry photograph. Four boys, Libra, Johnson, Crescent, and Vogney, standing beside a younger Britney Rellik and Pamela Darah, all in school jerseys. The girls looked stiff and unsmiling, as if they already knew a secret. The boys grinned smugly, untouchable, like the world was theirs.

"This is it!" Myrna revelled.

"Crescent left us the truth… or part of it."

"Or someone left it for us to find," Dessa said under her breath. Myrna turned to look at her.

"What do you mean?"

"Nothing," Dessa said quickly. "Just convenient, is all."

Myrna tucked the tin under her arm and stared at the mural again. She didn't say it aloud, but something in her gut agreed. This felt too well-placed, and yet… it still felt real.

"Let's run the photo through the system. I want names for anyone else in the background."

"On it," Dessa said.

"And I'll talk to the graffiti clean-up department. Maybe they have logs on who's been down here." They turned back toward the car. The city was quiet in that way, only late afternoon made possible, suspended, waiting. Myrna glanced back once more at the faded pink paint.

"Paint doesn't bleed,"

"No," Dessa said, opening the passenger door.

"But people do."

Back at the division, Myrna spread the contents of the tin across a clean desk. The doll arm, the half-melted chocolate kiss, the photograph, warped, but still legible. She slipped on gloves and placed them under the forensic scanner. Dessa angled closer to the photo,

"They look so young," she said in wonder.

"Too young to have done what they did," Myrna replied.

"And too smug not to get away with it."

Later that night, Myrna sat in the division's dimmed bullpen, the board looming silently across from her. She sipped lukewarm coffee, flipping through Crescent's coded journal again. The edges were smudged with graphite. The paper smelled like old cigarettes and river damp. Her eyes landed again on the phrase:

"They used to meet where the paint bled. B + P = Honeycomb."

Britney and Pamela, Commerce High, 1985. Cheerleading uniforms, Late-summer heat and secrets that still hadn't cooled. Myrna jotted a note: Check school archives for cheer squad rosters. '85–'86. She paused, looked at the blurry photograph again, the one from the tin. The girls were front and center. Pamela's smile was tight, like she didn't mean it.

Britney's hand rested possessively on her shoulder. Behind them, the boys grinned like they owned the world.

"They called themselves Honeycomb," Myrna whispered.

"Sweet on the outside, hollow in the middle." She hadn't meant to say it aloud. She flipped Crescent's journal to the last page again, the page with the line about drawings with no mouths, and Tuesdays. Crescent had written.

She said, he's next.

"But who was *she?*" Myrna asked no one. She scribbled more questions on a legal pad: Was Pamela the one Crescent saw? Was it Honeycomb together? Was someone else watching from the shadows, even then? She tapped her pen lightly against the desk, lips pressed into a tight line. Across the room, Dessa's side of the desk was empty. A cold teacup sat beside her chair. Myrna glanced at it briefly and looked away just as fast.

"Focus on the board," she whispered.

She turned back to the photo, circled Pamela and Britney's names, and underlined them twice. Then, she added a new question: What broke the honeycomb? Myrna stood and stretched. Tomorrow, they'd interview Britney again. And they'd dig deeper into Pamela's art, but tonight, all she could hear in her head was Crescent's voice, scrawled in pencil:

"She draws them with no mouths. But all she saw were mouths that never spoke, and names that refused to stay buried."

33

Bitters on the Tongue

Myrna sat on the edge of the sofa, her hands wrapped around a mug she hadn't sipped from in twenty minutes. Grant was eased back into the reclining section of the couch, nose-deep in a book.

"I feel like I'm being led," she confessed at last, her voice low.

Grant glanced up over the rim of his glasses.

"By whom?"

"The case, the evidence." Her gaze drifted to the mug as she set it down on the table, eyes following the thin ring it left on the wood.

"It's almost like someone's leaving breadcrumbs, not in a trail, but one by one, just enough to keep us thinking we're moving forward."

Grant closed his book and shifted beside her, the couch groaning under his weight.

"You think someone's feeding you the story they want you to believe."

"Exactly." Her hands laced together, restlessly twitching.

"And every time I start to see through it, something new drops in front of me: a clue, a photo, a name. It's too neat, too well-placed, or worse...planted."

For a moment, silence settled between them, broken only by the faint hum of a car passing. Then Grant spoke gently.

"So maybe the trick isn't to follow the trail, but to ask, who benefits from you following it?" Myrna's lips curved into a weary smile.

"You'd make a decent detective in another life."

"No thanks," he whispered, pressing a kiss against her temple.

"I'll stick with property law and brunch."

Her phone buzzed on the coffee table, the sound sharp in the quiet room. The screen lit up with a message from Dessa: Come in, you need to see this. Footage just pulled from Johnson's building. Myrna stood, slipping her phone into her hand with a sigh.

"Duty calls."

The image on the monitor was grainy, with fuzzed edges and static, but the timestamp glowed clear and cold: March 29th—6:41 p.m. Myrna and Dessa crowded into the AV room beside Mark, as the hum of machines filled the silence. Mark's fingers danced across the keyboard, scrubbing the footage backward, then forward again, until the camera caught the flicker of movement they were waiting for.

Onscreen, Harry Johnson came into view, leaning against the staff hallway entrance as though he had all the time in the world, hands loose in his pockets, posture lazy, a smirk practically implied. A heartbeat later, Stella Monet swept into frame, heels clicking on tile, a tailored coat cinched tight against her body, oversize sunglasses perched on her head like a tilted crown. Even blurred, she radiated presence.

The two met, and at first, it looked like small talk. Stella's head tilted, Harry's easy grin, but then her hand flew up, pressing against his chest. The casual mask slipped.

"Freeze that," Myrna said. The frame locked, catching Stella mid-motion, mouth open, her finger stabbing into Johnson's chest like a knife. Even in pixelated gray, her fury bled through.

"She's yelling," Dessa echoed, eyes narrowing.

"Not a sound feed in that wing," Mark said, shaking his head.

"Don't need one," Myrna replied quietly.

"Her body language screams plenty." Dessa stepped closer to the screen, thoughtful.

"Even so, we're guessing, we should get a lip reader on this. If she's making accusations or threats, we need it word-for-word. No jury buys body language alone."

Myrna stared at the frozen image, Stella's face twisted in fury. Johnson's hands raised defensively. A second later, the screen showed Stella storming away, her heel twisting slightly as she disappeared out of frame.

"Timestamp?" Myrna asked.

"6:48 p.m."

"And his time of death was estimated between 7 and 9," Dessa added.

Silence filled the room. Myrna's hands folded, chin on her knuckles.

"Stella said she hadn't seen Johnson in weeks," Dessa recalled.

"That's enough to haul her in, even if just to rattle her."

"Let's do it clean," Myrna agreed.

"Surprise visit. No warning." She looked at the image one more time before Mark minimized it. Something still didn't sit right. She wasn't sure if it was Stella, the footage, or the fact that the *bread crumb trail* had just conveniently extended itself again.

Back downstairs, Myrna stared at the whiteboard again, at Stella Monet's name now underlined in red. A thin line connected her to Harry Johnson, but it wasn't the line that bothered her. It was how fast it had been drawn.

"You seem tense," Dessa said, stepping into the room with two coffees.

"You ever get the feeling we're chasing shadows?" Myrna asked without looking up.

"We're always chasing shadows. That's the job."

Dessa set one of the coffees down and perched on the edge of her desk.

"But this," Myrna continued, gesturing to the timeline.

"This isn't just shadows, this is something else. Every time we hit a wall, the case opens up again, and something appears: a video, a photo, a journal, or a memory. Like we're being... spoon-fed the narrative." Dessa took a long sip, then shrugged.

"Or we're finally breaking through. You know how long we spent stalled. Maybe this is the payoff."

Myrna looked at her. Dessa's face was calm, maybe too quiet. There was no trace of doubt. No furrow in her brow.

"You're not even a little suspicious of how perfectly timed that surveillance footage was?"

"It was sitting in cold storage. Mark just missed the timestamp the first time," Dessa unrelenting. "It happens."

"Sure." Myrna, leaning back slowly.

Later that night, around midnight, Myrna sat at her kitchen table, a fresh notepad in front of her, not the official one, not department-issue, just hers. She opened it to a blank page and wrote at the top:

"What feels off?" She started a quiet list: Surveillance footage conveniently found. Photo and broken doll stashed under graffiti, too on-the-nose. Pamela's painting style is described in Crescent's journal, no real leads, only nudges.

She underlined the last point, then paused. It wasn't the evidence itself; it was the rhythm of it. Like someone was setting a pace, feeding just enough to keep them moving, but never enough to let them arrive. She tapped her pen, habitually, against the table.

"Someone wants us to see what they want us to see," she whispered. Myrna flipped back to an earlier page in the notebook. Re-read an old thought she'd jotted down a week ago:

"Clues aren't connecting, they're being connected."

It chilled her now in a way it hadn't before. She glanced at the time, almost 1 a.m. Outside, the city was hushed, but her thoughts weren't. She closed the notebook, slid it into her leather bag beneath her sidearm, and stood up.

"Keep walking forward," she flicked off the light.

"But start looking sideways."

34

The Honeycomb Pact

Stella Monet yanked the door open, a satin robe cinched carelessly at her waist, the fabric slipping just enough to suggest she hadn't bothered with anything underneath. Her hair was tousled, her eyes ringed with the smudges of cold cream, and her expression carried equal parts irritation and defiance.

"It's early," she muttered, her voice rough as gravel, though the clock in the hall behind her showed nearly noon. She stepped aside with a flick of her wrist, the sweet, cloying perfume wafting out into the hallway before either detective could say a word.

"Do you always show up uninvited, or is it just me you enjoy harassing?"

Myrna crossed the threshold first, her gaze sweeping the cramped apartment. The air was heavy with perfume and stale cigarettes, a messy jumble of silk cushions, empty glasses, and discarded heels scattered near the sofa.

"You lied to us," Myrna said flatly. Stella's shoulder caressed the doorframe as she tugged the robe tighter around herself, her mouth curling into a humourless smile.

"About what, detective?"

"You said you hadn't seen Johnson in weeks," Myrna continued, turning just enough to catch Stella's eye,

"But we have surveillance footage, dated and time-stamped, showing you arguing with him the very night he was murdered." Stella's smile faltered, but her eyes, sharp and watchful, never left Myrna's.

Dessa closed the door behind them, letting it click shut with a loud bang. Stella hesitated, her eyes darted toward the bathroom for a moment too long before she composed herself.

"Okay. Maybe I did see him. Maybe I told him to go to hell. That's not a crime."

"No, but lying to a homicide detective is," Myrna clipped, her tone landing like a gavel. Stella walked to her kitchen table and picked up a cup of coffee.

"I didn't kill him." She took a sip.

"You were furious. You shoved him." Myrna continued.

"He deserved worse," she snapped. "He used me, promised me a better life, then told me I wasn't good enough to bring around his army buddies." Dessa pulled out a chair from the table.

"You lived with him,"

"I needed a roof, he needed company. That's all it ever was."

She sat down beside Dessa, who now sat in the chair. Stella looked off into space, half frustrated, half melancholy. Myrna noticed her eyes and, for the first time, saw some humanity in Stella Monet.

"Where were you between seven and nine that night?" Myrna pressed. Stella rolled her eyes.

"Working at the Diamonds Cabaret Club, check the tapes."

Dessa scribbled the name into her notebook.

"We will," she said. Myrna took one last look around the cramped apartment, eyes lingering on a red stiletto tipped over near the hallway. Something about the whole place felt like a carefully curated disaster.

"We'll be in touch."

By the time the sun shifted west, they were back at Ottawa P.D., Interview Room One. Pamela Darah sat across from them, a black turtleneck clinging like armour, her fingers stained faintly with charcoal.

"I already told you," she said calmly, "I didn't know those men." Myrna sat down.

"Except you were seen at Charles Libra's funeral,"

"I study expressions, raw grief, anger, it fascinates me. I sketch what I see, it's not illegal."

"And yet your photo was found on Libra's computer," Dessa added. Pamela blinked once.

"I didn't send it."

"Your name came up again and again, even in Johnson's emails." Pamela's mouth twisted slightly, looking right at Dessa.

"You think I did it? Then search my studio. Go ahead, it's on Preston, second floor. The keys are in my bag."

The detectives exchanged a glance, surprised by the offer.

"Tell us about Honeycomb," Dessa said solemnly.

"Gee, haven't heard that word in years," Pamela said, easing forward.

"You and Britney Rellik used that name in high school. You two were close?" Dessa questioned, and Pamela hesitated.

"We were something that was a long time ago."

"Honeycomb, some sort of pact?" Myrna said, watching

Pamela's face closely. Pamela flinched, just slightly.

"We were kids."

"Kids with a secret?" Dessa reacted. Pamela sat back in her chair.

"Search the studio. I have nothing to hide."

Dessa closed the distance between them, her eyes locked on Pamela like a hawk ready to strike. She could feel the moment tipping, the fragile pause before confession. Her voice was low but insistent, coaxing and cornering at once.

"Come on, Pamela," she pressed, every syllable deliberate.

"Tell us what happened back in 1985. What was the pact about?"

The room seemed to hold its breath. Dessa waited, her anticipation building, convinced Darah was about to crack; the truth was balanced on the edge of her lips. But when the silence broke, the voice that cut through the air didn't belong to Pamela Darah at all. It was sharp, ragged, almost desperate.

"Stop!" Johnathan Karamel's shout ricocheted through the room, shattering the moment like glass.

Myrna winced, knowing it was over.

"She's not under arrest." Karamel laid his briefcase on the table.

"Detective, you know that you should not be talking with my client without me present." Pamela looked at him, puzzled.

"I don't mind talking to them. I am not a murderer,"

"Miss Darah, I've told you that is not an option without me present," Karamel responded, still angry, he walked toward the door, motioning for Pamela to follow.

Hours later, after Pamela's lawyer shut down the interview, the detectives moved quickly. A warrant in hand, they seized the chance to comb through Pamela's art studio. The place was exactly what they expected: concrete floors, splattered canvases, the heavy scent of turpentine and varnish, soft light filtered through frosted windows. Faces stared from every wall, distorted, haunting, beautiful.

Dessa sifted through a stack of sketchbooks.

"She wasn't lying," she whispered.

"They're all emotion. Some of them were screaming." Myrna crossed the room, yanking open drawers, finding nothing but half-used tubes of paint. She crouched, pulled at a crate, only to uncover more blank canvases stacked like shields. Frustration edged her breath. Then, at the back of a narrow cabinet, her fingers brushed fabric, a silk scarf. Wrapped inside was a small leather-bound pink book. The first few pages were drawings, angry lines, mostly faces without mouths. Then, near the center: words, journal entries, dated, personal and dark.

One read:

"He laughed when I said no. They all laughed. But I kept the wrappers; every one."

"We need this logged and bagged," Myrna said anxiously. Dessa turned and walked in her direction.

"You think this was written before or after the murders started?" She asked.

"I think it was meant to be found." Dessa opened an evidence bag, and Myrna dropped the diary inside.

"Well, let's get it to the lab. We'll know more once it's analyzed."

By evening, the detectives shifted to Interview Room Two. Britney Rellik sat with her fingers combing through her fiery red curls as she pulled them into a tight ponytail, as if she didn't trust them to behave. Her face was flushed with anger or nerves; it was hard to tell.

"I don't know what Pamela told you, but I haven't spoken with her in what, eight or nine years?" Avoids eye contact.

"Time flies when you're pretending nothing ever happened."

Myrna looked up curiously.

"What do you mean?" Britney didn't respond; instead, she hung her head shamefully.

"The Honeycomb Pact," Myrna continued,

"What does that mean? What is it exactly?"

"Back in high school? We were... inseparable, best friends, cheerleaders and secret-keepers. Everyone thought we were just bright, sweet, popular girls." She gave a brittle laugh.

"They didn't see how sharp we were. How mean, sometimes, cunning, even, more than people gave us credit for."

"The hive, that was Pamela's idea. Bees, loyal to the queen, protect the hive no matter what. That's how we saw ourselves. Stupid, maybe, but it felt real back then."

"You mess with one of us, you mess with the hive."

"So were there more cheerleaders a part of the hive?" Dessa interjected. Britney smiled slightly,

"They all were, but only Pamela and I were part of the pact." Myrna's patience was wearing thin.

"What pact?"

Britney folded her lips and clasped her hands on the table.

"The Honeycomb Pact... yeah. That was after... something happened to Pamela. Summer '85. I don't..." She stopped, twisting her hands.

"It was before senior year. Everything shifted after that." Dessa placed her face into her palm, rubbing her temples with her thumb and index finger.

"Where did this happen?"

"It was at a cottage west of Ottawa, Cala something."

"Was it Calabogie?" Myrna suggested.

"Yes, that's it." Britney reacted with a revelation.

Myrna sat closer to Britney, placing her hand on her shoulder to appear empathetic.

"I know this must be difficult to talk about. Please tell us about the incident." Britney shook her head,

"I wasn't there. I was supposed to go, but my parents said no. Boy was I mad, but in retrospect, grateful."

Myrna squeezed her shoulder,

"Please continue." Britney used two fingers to fix a loose curl behind her ear.

"We swore to never speak of it, to keep our silence sealed in wax."

"We called this vow the Honeycomb Pact, a private promise to each other to protect ourselves at all costs. It became a form of survival, a secret code between us that no one else could break."

"But you said that you weren't there," Dessa said in confirmation.

"No, I wasn't assaulted, but I had my demons or reasons for protection. Pamela didn't go into details; she confirmed that she was raped at the cottage, but she wouldn't go to the police, her parents or say who did it."

Dessa looked at her strangely,

"So what happened between you two?" Britney shrugs,

"I don't know. It started when I was dating Johnson. However brief that was, she acted as if he were a plague or something, and resented me for being with him. Got even worse when I reconnected with Vogney."

"You never thought to report this to the police," Myrna shaking her head in disbelief.

"She wouldn't even talk to me, let alone a strange cop."

"She was too ashamed of what had happened to her, I don't know why, but she blamed herself. No matter how many times I told her it wasn't her fault, she never believed me.

Dessa's chair screeched back against the floor. She shot up, arms crossing tight, then falling open in disbelief. Her jaw worked as though she might swallow her own words, but they burst out anyway.

"Wo... wow."

She shook her head hard, storming toward the door. Myrna gave her a beat, then followed. Out in the hall, Dessa stood rigid, fists clenched, eyes hot.

"You mind telling me what the hell that was about?"

"That bitch is as dense as a brick wall."

Myrna closed her eyes and folded her head into her right palm.

"Dessa, you have got to calm down." Too upset to listen, she shook her head briskly.

"It's bad enough that she didn't report it, but she screws the two guys that raped her best friend, then wonders why the woman's pissed." Myrna's two palms go up in an attempt to quiet Dessa.

"Settle down, she might hear you."

"I don't give a shit!"

"OK, you're done, walk away." Myrna pointed toward their desk. Dessa turned and walked away.

Back inside the interview room, Myrna reminded Britney to speak the truth when talking about Crescent.

"We know that you didn't just meet him once at the hospital

and have security toss him. Help yourself here, Britney. Pamela is looking good in these murders. Decide if you want to go down with her."

Britney took a deep breath.

"What do you want to know?"

"What do you know about Crescent?"

"He was younger and not fully part of the group, but watched from the edges and tried hard to fit in. He idolized Pamela and followed her around." Myrna flips a page in her notebook. "What about writing in journals?"

"He was always scribbling in some book; I have no idea what he wrote. I tell you what, though, Pamela would."

35

Kisses in Code

The division was quiet that evening, the kind of quiet Myrna Watkis had come to recognize, not as peace, but as pressure. It settled over the squad room like a blanket, making every tick of the wall clock sound louder than necessary. She sat alone at her desk, Pamela Darah's diary spread out in front of her, gloved fingers turning its fragile pages. The ink smelled faintly fresh, too fresh.

Dessa was off getting a report from tech, leaving Myrna a rare moment of stillness and clarity. She reached for her black notebook, the one she kept separate from the case files, and jotted down:

- *Darah's diary: no fingerprints. Fresh ink. Latex residue.*
- *Why no defensive stance from her?*
- *Was it planted — and if so, by whom?*

She tapped the pen against the desk, sharp, rhythmic, impatient. She circled Pamela Darah's name, then stopped. No check mark this time. Just a question mark, bold and lonely on the page.

Dessa returned with a thin file in hand and a paper coffee cup in the other. She dropped the file on Myrna's desk. Myrna looked up, astonished.

"Girl, another cup of coffee? You're gonna make Tim Horton's rich." Dessa smiled warmly,

"I brought you your favourite cherry doughnut, no coffee."

"Now, you're talking." Dessa laughed heartily.

"What you got there?" Myrna asked.

"Forensics on the diary and wrappers, you're not going to like it." Myrna flipped it open.

- *No fingerprints found on the book.*
- *Traces of powdered latex — consistent with glove residue were detected on the leather.*
- *The chocolate kiss wrappers glued inside came from a limited-edition seasonal batch, only available last winter, well after Libra's and Johnson's murders.*

"So Pamela couldn't have left them at the original crime scenes," Myrna spoke softly.

"Or she's reusing the same signature now," Dessa said flatly. Myrna's brow furrowed.

"Dessa, it doesn't make sense. She gave us the key. Why would she offer up her studio if she were hiding that kind of evidence?"

"Because to her, it's not evidence," Dessa replied.

"It's art, performance. Half those canvases seemed to scream, remember? What's one more scream, dressed up as a diary?"

Myrna didn't answer, but kept the idea of someone staging the scene, someone with access to the art studio, someone arrogant enough to leave notes at crime scenes without detection, in the back of her mind. She wrote another line in her notebook: *We're not uncovering. We're being led.*

Later that afternoon, Dr. Festus met them outside the lab, his glasses sliding down his nose as he handed over a report sheet.

"Thought you'd want to see this in person," he said.

"Crescent's toxicology results came back strange."

"Strange how? Myrna inquired, In addition to arsenic and whatever toxic cocktail you found in his stomach?"

"We picked up a varnish-based compound in his lungs and throat. The kind used in oil painting, or to preserve charcoal."

Dessa raised her eyebrows.

"You're kidding."

"I never kid about varnish," Festus replied dryly. Myrna snapped the report shut.

"Could someone have poured it down his throat postmortem?"

"Unlikely. This was inhaled. It was either aerosolized or misted; he choked on it before he died."

"Like pepper spray," Dessa added.

"Or paint fumes," Myrna said quietly, staring off.

That night, Myrna sat cross-legged on her sofa, laptop closed beside her, diary notes spread across her coffee table. The division lights were long behind her, but the mental murk was still thick. In her secret notebook, she made a list:

All four victims:

- Libra: strangled, staged
- Johnson: shot, embalmed
- Vogney: heart attack, crash
- Crescent: poisoned, sketched on

Then:

All crime scenes:

- Symbolic
- Gendered
- Misdirection
- Always—performative

She underlined twice: *Someone is staging a story, but not their own.* She paused, then wrote one more sentence: *Someone wants Pamela blamed, someone who has reason to hate her.* The next morning, a tech from Evidence arrived at her desk with a brown envelope.

"Found this in a mattress at the shelter. It's the rest of Crescent's journal. Someone shoved it between the coils. We missed it in the first sweep."

Myrna turned another page, the paper brittle beneath her gloves. At first, it looked like more ramblings, jagged words crawling across the margin. Then her breath caught.

A face stared back at her. It was crudely pencilled, the lines smudged as though Crescent had drawn it in the dark, obsessively, over and over. The eyes were the worst of it; wide, unblinking, intense. Not Pamela's, not Britney's, not Stella or Belinda. Yet something about the tilt of the jaw, the set of the mouth, nagged at her like a half-remembered dream.

The girl wore a wide-brimmed hat, brim shadowing her hair, erasing the details that might have betrayed who she was. Race, age, even the exact expression blurred in the graphite haze, as if Crescent wanted her both known and unknowable.

Below the sketch, a single line scrawled in sporadic handwriting:

Queen of the Hive.

Myrna sat frozen, staring at the image. She wasn't recognized yet, but it was someone, and Crescent had crowned her at the center of everything. Something about this was wrong, terribly wrong. Her pulse quickened as her mind reached back, grasping at fragments of Crescent's journal.

A bloodless oath, two bees were sworn to silence. One sting, and the hive goes down. The words crawled into her thoughts like a whisper from the grave. Her stomach dropped. This wasn't about the girls at all. The chilling metaphor, so carefully hidden in Crescent's handwriting, pointed elsewhere, toward the men. And if the oath was real, then someone had already broken it.

36

Foil and Fragments

The snow fell thick and slow, softening the city's edges. The twinkling lights on trees and buildings, illuminated wreaths, garland and colourful banners, combined with the sounds of joyous Christmas songs, created a festive atmosphere. For once, Ottawa seemed to exhale, a contrast to the heaviness and despair that came with the chaos of a crime scene.

Dessa stood outside her brother Darren's townhouse, both hands filled with overstuffed shopping bags. Through the frosted front window, she could already see her sisters bickering over oven space. Her sister-in-law, Noelle, had bravely offered to host Christmas. Having prior knowledge of her sisters, Dessa had pledged to defend Noelle at all costs. It would seem she was just in time.

The door burst open before she could knock. Her niece ran past her older cousin and flung her arms around Dessa's waist. From the look on Joshua's face, she knew Grandma was having a good day.

"Come here, you." Auntie's arms were wide open. Joshua hugged Dessa, displaying a dimpled smile.

"You're late," said Deshauna, wiping her hands on a Christmas-themed apron dusted with flour and streaks of butter.

"If the ham is dry, it's your fault." Dessa rolled her eyes, leaned in to kiss her mother's cheek, and stepped across the threshold. Warmth rushed at her, cinnamon and nutmeg lacing the air, a sharp jerk of spice curling against the softer scent of baked ham. Her boots squeaked against linoleum dusted faintly with flour, and light glinted off tinsel that kept slipping from the bannister; imperfect, but stubbornly festive. Beneath it all was the deeper, unspoken scent of home: love stretched thin, but never broken.

The house pulsed with life. In the kitchen, Dianne's voice rose above the clatter of serving spoons as she loudly critiqued the potato salad for being too heavy on the mayo. Her husband, Marcus, stirred the gravy like it was a science experiment, repeating,

"It's fine, Di," only to earn a sharp look that dared him to keep talking.

Deshauna, younger but endlessly bossy, swanned about in a velvet dress, her smug smile as carefully arranged as the platters she kept straightening, undoing Noelle's careful work to redo it again. Terrence leaned against the counter with a glass of rum and eggnog, shaking his head with an amused grin.

"You're all acting like this is the World Cup of ham. I'm just here for the black cake." In the living room, Darren had achieved his usual diplomatic invisibility, sprawled across the couch in a half-doze as Deshauna's daughter climbed him like a jungle gym, her giggles mixing with the carols playing faintly from the stereo.

Every corner brimmed with motion, cutlery clinking, a door slamming upstairs, bursts of laughter that threatened to tip into bickering. It was chaos, but it was theirs.

Into the kitchen, Dessa went, expecting to put out metaphoric fires. She tasted the potato salad,

"Hmm, so good, I need the recipe." She smiled, staring straight at Dianne. Noelle hugged her, whispering lightly,

"Thank you, you're awesome."

"Wow, you look about ready to pop," she said, looking down at Noelle's belly.

Later, during dinner, her mother turned to her with a look that seemed to know too much.

"You've got shadows in your eyes, baby girl. Don't let them follow you into the new year." Dessa gave her a tired smile and excused herself. She helped her nephew finish a 100-piece puzzle in the quiet den, fingers tracing over the missing corners. Her nephew pressed the last puzzle piece into place, a corner missing from the picture. The glossy surface caught the lamplight and twinkled like tinsel. Dessa leaned closer, her reflection split across the cardboard.

"Funny how you can lose one little piece," she uttered, voice soft enough her nephew didn't notice.

"And the whole picture feels wrong."

He laughed, already reaching for the box lid, but Dessa kept staring at the gap, her smile frozen, as though it reminded her of something she couldn't afford to say aloud.

Myrna stood nervously beside Grant, adjusting the buttons of his coat as they walked up her parents' driveway. The lights were modest, tasteful. Everything, as always, was just right. Her mother, Gwen, greeted them at the door with a hug slightly too firm and a smile that was a little too excited.

"Grant," she said brightly.

"You sell houses, right? I've been thinking about listing the cottage in Arnprior."

"I'd be happy to take a look," Grant said with practiced charm. Her father, Peter, emerged from the den and shook Grant's hand, ushering him into a quiet conversation about property taxes and the Jays' season.

The roast was already in the oven, the vegetables were chopped, and everything was prepared. Even the place cards on the table had been printed. Dinner passed in elegant courses: salad, soup, main, but Myrna barely tasted it. At one point, she caught her younger cousin trying to flirt with Grant over dessert. He didn't notice, but she did.

As her mother raised a toast,

"To a new year with big changes," Myrna's smile froze. Alone in the powder room, she traced a fingertip across the cool porcelain, her reflection watching back from the gilt-edged mirror. The toast's words still rang in her ears: *big changes.* Myrna forced a smile at the glass, one she didn't believe in, and whispered,

"You can't have everything." Then she turned off the light, carrying the shadow of it back to the table.

Downtown Ottawa – December 31

The condo buzzed with warmth. Grant's place, high up on the twelfth floor, had a view of the city lights shimmering like sequins under a velvet sky. String lights were draped across the windows. Someone had lit candles that smelled like peppermint and cedarwood.

Dessa arrived in a fitted red dress, Bartlett beside her in a crisp navy suit. They carried champagne and laughter in equal measure. Music filled the room: Marvin Gaye, a little Etta James, a few curveballs thrown in from Dessa's playlist. Grant grilled steaks on the balcony with Bartlett under the heater lamp, while the women raided the cookie tray inside.

"We deserve this," Myrna declared, mouth full.

"One night where nobody dies."

"Knock on wood," Dessa replied, tapping her forehead.

"We've still got two hours." Time passed slowly. It was the kind of night that felt borrowed, no talk of murder and no case boards, just clinks of glasses and warmth in the bones. At 11:45, they stood outside on the balcony. The air was sharp but invigorating. Below them, the city flickered with anticipation.

"You think this next year's gonna be better?" Bartlett asked.

"Define better," Dessa quipped, leaning into his side.

"Less blood," Myrna said, smiling thinly.

"More answers," Grant added, slipping an arm around her waist. When the countdown started, they returned to the living room.

"Ten... nine... eight..."

Grant kissed Myrna gently as the numbers dropped. Bartlett grinned and dipped Dessa low into a dramatic kiss. Fireworks erupted outside the windows, bursts of light chasing away a year of darkness.

"Three... two... one..."

The room rang with cheers, sparkling wine, and the faint scent of sandalwood and ambergris. Fireworks faded into smoke outside the glass, but the smell of smoke and champagne clung to the room. Laughter still rippled, glasses still clinked, yet Myrna caught Dessa's gaze across the couch, a flicker, too fast to name. The night was warm, borrowed.

Tomorrow would not be.

37

Shards of Sweetness

The sun had barely climbed over the horizon when Myrna Watkis found herself back in the squad room, staring at Crescent's battered journal in front of her. She'd flipped past the scrawlings and madness more times than she could count, but today she lingered on one sketch, burned in her mind like a branding iron. The sketch wasn't new to her; she'd studied it before, but today the eyes seemed to follow her, sharper, more accusing. *Queen of the Hive.* A girl's face, maybe fifteen, with wide-set eyes and a narrow jawline. She'd shown it to no one, not yet, not even Dessa.

The female's face was hard to place, but it *was* familiar, the eyes, especially, and the tilt of the jaw. Myrna flipped back through Crescent's pages, incoherent ramblings filled the margins:

She leads them. Honey sticks to her fingers. She never forgets.

She looked up when Dessa came in casually, tossing her keys on the desk.

"Any resemblance you can place?" Dessa paused for a minute.

"Maybe one of the suspects? Maybe Sue." Myrna bent down under her desk to pick up her fallen pen.

"Not sure, Sue is the answer, but she looks like I've seen her before."

Dessa tossed her coffee cup in the bin and picked up the book. She pulled it closer, studying the girl's face intently.

"How do you think she relates to the ramblings: leads, honey, never forgets?"

"I'm not sure, that's why I made an appointment with the forensic psychologist." Dessa lowered the book,

"Oh? When do we go?"

"We don't, she's on her way."

"I need someone who can read between the lines. Someone who understands how a disturbed mind tries to confess without really confessing."

Dr. Elaine Mercer, a seasoned forensic psychologist in her mid-50s, entered the division and was directed to the detective's desk. Detective Watkis stood up and shook her hand.

"Dr. Mercer, good to see you again. Thanks for taking the time. I know it's short notice."

"No trouble at all, what are we looking at?" Myrna gestured to a chair.

"Something different. A collection of journal entries. Ramblings, written by a man named Larry Crescent. He's not the suspect, but he might be the key to understanding someone who is."

Dr. Mercer sat in the chair provided.

"Psychological projection? Codependency? Or are we talking

something more cryptic, manifestos, delusions?"

"A bit of all three, maybe. The language is poetic, obsessive. He talks about a honeycomb pact, makes references to fire, purity, shame, secrets... It's dense. Thought you could help me make sense of it, what kind of mind we're dealing with, and who he might've been protecting."

Myrna placed her palm on her forehead with a small tap, looking at Dessa.

"Where are my manners? Dr. Mercer, this is my partner, Dessa Simms."

"Nice to meet you." Dr. Mercer took the book.

"Let's see what the subconscious has to say. People reveal more between the lines than they think."

The doctor paused for a time, reading the pages slowly.

"He saw the others, Libra, Johnson, Vogney, even himself, as bees orbiting her. After the assault, it's as if she haunted them, influencing their fates. His guilt mutated into the belief she was in control. In his delusion, *she leads them* means she was the beginning of their end."

Myrna and Dessa shared a look. For a moment, she felt like one of those bees Mercer had described; circling, restless, compelled toward the center. Dessa, tapping her pen against the page, was no better: buzzing with questions, drawn closer by each fragment of Crescent's madness. The queen might have been a phantom in a sketch, but already she was pulling them into her hive.

Mercer turned another page.

"*Honey sticks to her fingers* signals obsession and fixation, a kind of personified guilt. In Crescent's damaged mind, sweetness and shame fused until desire itself became incriminating. She was magnetic, irresistible, but dangerous: the sweetness clings, it leaves a mark, it attracts bees, and it attracts trouble."

Myrna's pen stilled. Even the metaphor felt sticky, cloying. Mercer's voice softened.

"*She never forgets* is the most unambiguous shard, a pure projection of his fear. Survivors encode memory differently. Crescent externalized that certainty: the past will not dissolve."

She set the journal down.

"Each line is a fragment, a shard of sweetness broken off from one terrible memory. Together, they form a pattern, his fear that the past has sharpened itself into judgment."

"Crescent, in his drunken spiral of guilt and paranoia, knows someone remembers what they did, and he projects that certainty onto the girl. In his eyes, she never forgot. She held onto the pain. Maybe she's coming for them. Maybe she already did. And that's why she becomes *Queen of the Hive*, the survivor who remembers when all the others tried to forget."

Dr. Mercer closed the journal gently, her fingers lingering on the worn cover.

"This isn't just guilt speaking. It's fear, and the belief, true or not, that the past has come back to collect. Fragments of something once pure, now sharpened by time and buried beneath layers of silence and shame."

The room fell silent. Myrna glanced at Dessa, who had stopped writing, her pen suspended mid-air.

"She's alive,"

Myrna tapped the desk. Dessa's brow furrowed.

"You think the girl from the sketch... she survived?"

"No,"

Myrna interjected, her eyes locked on the face in the drawing.

"I think she remembered."

Dr. Mercer looked between them, her voice calm but weighted.

"Whoever she is, she's not done with them. Or with you."

Myrna stood slowly and picked up the sketch.

"Then it's time we found out who the Queen of the Hive is. And this time, she'd show her face to everyone."

38

Dark Chocolate

The morning light filtered through the blinds in thin, dusty strips. Myrna stood at the whiteboard, marker in hand, staring at the grid of names, arrows, and photos as if they were part of an ancient puzzle that was only now beginning to take shape.

"She remembered," she whispered again, circling the phrase at the center: Queen of the Hive.

Dessa stood in the doorframe, her expression tight.

"You've been staring at that board for an hour."

"I did a side-by-side with that sketch. Pulled old yearbooks, news clippings, and school photos. No match, not directly, anyway."

Myrna didn't look away from the board.

"That's because we've been looking at girls we knew were there. But what if she wasn't in the photo? What if she wasn't supposed to be there at all?"

Dessa blinked.

"An outsider?"

Myrna nodded slowly.

"A shadow on the edge of the frame."

"We need to search Pamela Darah's studio again. Not just for evidence, for intention. If someone wanted her framed as the Queen, maybe they left us something more."

Detectives entered Pamela's Art Studio later that morning. Pamela had been making hot chocolate, and the scent lingered in the air, rich and bittersweet, like a secret left behind. The irony was not lost on Myrna. The second search was quiet, no quips, no bravado, just dust, silence, and charcoal ghosts staring from the walls. The cold air felt alive in the room, like the walls were holding their breath. The light slanted sharply across the floor, illuminating a cut-up doll torso beneath a worktable. Its plastic limbs were severed, the inside stuffed with shreds of foil candy wrappers. The foil caught in Myrna's gloves, crinkling like laughter in an empty room.

Dessa bent down slowly, her breath catching in her throat. "Kisses..." Myrna crouched beside her, eyes narrowing on the warped toy. The foil wrappers glinted under the dim light, like confetti from a child's nightmare.

"It's almost like she wanted us to find this," Myrna echoed.

"Or... someone wanted us to."

They pushed deeper into the cluttered studio, canvases and toolboxes looming like silent witnesses. The air grew heavier the farther they went, every step kicking up the musk and dust.

In the back alcove, behind a leaning easel, Myrna froze. Her hand hovered over the wall, a faint seam, unnatural, deliberate. "Here."

She whispered, prying the panel open. The cavity yawned wide. Inside, dozens of faces stared back at them, cut from glossy magazines, edges charred black as though kissed by flame. They were arranged in uneven rows, tight and claustrophobic, like cells in a honeycomb, a hive built of ash and memory. Uneasy, Myrna flashed back to a half-memory of her grandmother's bee stories.

Beneath each one, a name, scrawled in angry strokes: Libra, Johnson, Vogney, Crescent, and more. Dessa's voice cracked.

"There's more?" Myrna rose slowly, her face grim.

"This isn't art," she said, the words sticking like ash.

"This is a ritual."

On Pamela's workbench, they found another journal. Not pink. This one was black, hardbound, with silver lettering that had been half-scratched off. They flipped through it cautiously. It was full of sketches and pages of mirrored writing. One page stopped them cold:

"You can kill a bee, but the hive always remembers."

Later that afternoon, back at the division. The evidence board was full, too full. Faces, timelines, and Post-it notes cluttered in every shade of desperation. Myrna tapped the marker in the palm of her hand.

"We're not just chasing a killer," Myrna said.

"We're chasing someone who knows how to plant doubt, how to make us stare at the wrong things at the right time. And now we're left with a board full of lies pressed together like bittersweet shards, impossible to swallow."

39

Melted Truths

The city was buried beneath thick snow that draped the ground in heavy, uneven drifts, softening the sharp angles of sidewalks and rooftops into quiet mounds. Trees stood cloaked in frost, their bare branches laced with silver, like veins of ice stretched across the sky. Every breath turned to mist, hanging in the air before vanishing into the cold.

In the distance, a snowplow groaned its way down the street, carving paths through the whiteness, only for them to begin filling again almost as quickly. Footprints were few, and already half-erased by fresh flurries. The city felt still, like nature was holding its breath beneath a frozen spell.

Myrna and her partner pulled up to an apartment building on Bank Street. Dessa killed the engine, drumming her fingers against the steering wheel.

"She's not gonna like seeing us again." Myrna didn't look up from her notepad.

"She doesn't have to like it. She only has to tell the truth. And remember, the melted truth wasn't found in warmth or sunlight, but in the quiet cracks beneath cold smiles and colder intentions. People don't only speak with words."

The lobby smelled faintly of boiled cabbage and lemon cleaner. Myrna took the lead, her boots thudding up the narrow staircase. Dessa followed, scanning the walls lined with dated wallpaper and yellowed crown moulding.

"You think she's gonna talk this time?"

"She talked last time,"

"She just didn't realize how much."

On the third floor, they stopped in front of unit 3B. The wooden door bore fresh scratches around the lock and a dent low on the frame, like someone had once tried to kick it in. Myrna knocked. There was a pause. Then, the soft click of a deadbolt. Sue opened the door, wearing plaid pyjama pants and a Bob Marley T-shirt with the sleeves cut off.

Her braids were pinned up, piled messily on her head with a claw clip, and her eyes were sharp despite the casual clothes. A smudge of eyeliner had settled beneath one lid, like she'd slept in yesterday's makeup. She looked at them with the weary irritation of someone who'd been hoping the knock was food delivery.

"Well, shit," she said flatly.

"You two again."

"Good morning to you, too," Dessa replied, stepping forward. Sue blocked the door frame and didn't open it wider.

"It's my day off, what now?"

"We just need a few minutes," Myrna said calmly.

"You mentioned something before, about a girl. We'd like you to clarify."

Sue studied them for a minute, then sighed and stepped aside.

"Fine. But no shoes on the carpet. I just vacuumed."

The apartment inside was small but cozy, walls painted a deep, moody green, showing a thrift-store chic vibe: mismatched lamps, a cat asleep on a windowsill, and a turntable spinning quietly in the corner. Vinyl records propped against one wall like fallen dominoes. The scent of jasmine incense hung in the air.

She motioned to the couch, which sagged in the middle.

"Sit if you want, I need coffee if I'm going to be remembering ghosts."

Myrna and Dessa's eyes met briefly across the room. Something about Sue, the brittle calm, the practiced nonchalance, told them today might finally crack something open.

"You mentioned once that Larry talked about a girl. You said her name was Kamala."

Sue frowned,

"Yeah, or Pamela, I don't know. His words came out bent."

"You said whatever happened between them was why he drank," Dessa added.

"Do you remember anything else?" Sue looked away, toward the window where the sunlight leaked in over frostbitten geraniums.

"Just that she was young, like, too young. He felt guilty, I think. Said they'd all laughed at her."

"Who's 'they'?" Myrna asked quietly.

"He never said names, but I think it was more than one guy. He said she cried, and nobody gave a damn. Called her the Queen Bee or something, like it was a joke, but his face," she stopped, voice cracking.

"It wasn't a joke to him."

"Did he say where it happened?" Dessa shot her a look, pointed, and skeptical.

"Cottage... summer?"

Sue chewed on a fingernail.

"Somewhere up north, cottage, yeah. Maybe Bogie, Calabogie. I remember because I thought it sounded made-up." Myrna flipped her notebook shut.

"You said he started drinking around that time?"

"No," Sue shook her head,

"He was already drinking, but it got worse after he ran into one of them again. A guy, I don't know who. He saw him at a corner store, or something, came home shaking."

Myrna and Dessa looked at each other, unspoken thoughts passing between them.

"You never mentioned that before." Sue shrugged.

"Didn't think it mattered. Thought he was, just, seeing ghosts." For a long moment, no one spoke, then Myrna said,

"Do you know when that was, when he saw the guy again?"

Sue tilted her head.

"A few months before he died, maybe? Winter, I think, but don't quote me."

As they stood to leave, Myrna paused.

"Last question, have you ever heard him use the phrase honeycomb?" Sue blinked.

"Yeah... he said it once. Thought it was code for something. *Hive mind,* he mumbled. *No escape from the honeycomb.* It scared the hell out of me, to be honest."

Dessa scribbled fast. Myrna stared ahead, eyes rigid. Outside, the snow moved with the wind, blowing briskly through the air, like the last of someone's secrets.

"She didn't give us anything new," Dessa said, holding a grim expression.

"That whole 'Kamala' thing still feels like a dead end."

"Not quite," Myrna opened the car door and sat down.

"She remembered enough to show that Larry was carrying guilt. That drawing haunted him. Whoever the girl is, he kept seeing her."

"We need to talk with Pamela; she is the one person who can shed light on this girl's identity."

"What makes you think Pamela isn't the girl, or attached to her in some way, and by extension, the killer?" Dessa threw her hand up in the air, waiting for Myrna's response.

"Dessa, I'm just not convinced; all the evidence against her is too convenient. What I do know for sure is that she was victimized, and getting her to admit that is the first step to finding the girl in the sketch."

Dessa conceded,

"O.K., how do you want to do this?"

"It's early in the day, she's probably at her studio. Let's go there, less risk of running into Karamel." Dessa pulled out her keys from her pocket.

"You really think she's going to, just admit she was attacked?"

"She's come close," Myrna defended.

"And I don't think she knows who the girl in the sketch is... not consciously. But if we can get her to talk, really talk, maybe she'll remember."

"Or maybe she's just playing us both," Dessa rubbed her hands together, blowing hot breath into her palms.

"You trust people too easily."

"And you don't trust them at all." Dessa smiles.

"And that's what keeps me alive." The vehicle pulled out of the parking spot, engine humming heavily, snow rustling beneath the tires. A silence settled between them as Myrna tried to focus on the road.

"Look," she finally said, quietly.

"You think Pamela's the killer. I think she's another victim. But either way, we're not going to know the truth unless we ask the right questions."

"And if she runs?"

"Then we'll know she has something to hide."

The door was open. Pamela stood in ripped jeans and an oversized sweater, her hair knotted in a messy bun, and black smudges dusted her cheekbones. She looked startled, but only for a second.

"I thought you were done bothering me," she said, stepping away from the painting she was working on.

"We said we'd be in touch," Myrna replied, as she walked around.

Dessa followed, quiet for once. Pamela's studio was even more cluttered than last time. New canvases settled against the walls. Faces stared from every surface, twisted, beautiful, mouths still absent.

"I'm not under arrest, am I?" Pamela asked dryly, wiping her hands on a paint-smeared rag.

"No," answered Myrna.

"We just have some questions. Personal ones." Pamela's forehead wrinkled, a slight twitch of a nostril.

"You want tea or answers first?"

"Answers," Dessa said. Myrna held out a sheet of paper. On it was a photocopy of Crescent's sketch, the girl labelled Queen of the Hive. Pamela looked at it, then squinted.

"That's not me."

"You're sure?" Dessa asked, head cocked, a skeptical edge in her voice.

"You were younger once."

Pamela stared at the image longer than necessary.

"I've never looked like this," she said, but a hitch caught in her voice.

"If you look closely at the style of the sketch, it could be interpreted as a Black female. The cap she is wearing covers her hair." Dessa looked at her, almost angry. We can see the lack of shading could be interpreted as a Caucasian female, as well.

"We showed it to Sue," Myrna said.

"She wasn't sure either. But she remembered Larry Crescent mentioning a name once, Kamala." Pamela flinched, almost invisibly.

"Was he talking about you?" Myrna pressed.

"Or someone else?"

Pamela turned her back, walking toward a nearby easel.

"Why are we going over this again?"

"Because it matters," Myrna said gently.

"That girl... she's the origin of all this. The beginning of the spiral. We need to know who she is." Pamela was silent for a long time.

Dessa rolled her eyes sarcastically.

"Let me guess. You're going to say you don't remember the summer of 1985 either." Pamela glanced over her shoulder.

"I remember enough."

"Then say it," Dessa snapped.

"Say what happened." The room fell still. Pamela turned around, her voice low.

"We were kids, some of us more than others."

"You were sixteen," Myrna said. Pamela nodded.

"And?" Dessa's eyes narrowed.

"Say it."

"I don't need to perform my trauma for you," Pamela snapped sharply.

"What difference does it make now?" Myrna stepped closer to Pamela, placing her hands on her shoulder.

"It makes all the difference. Pamela, you weren't the only one hurt. Crescent wasn't just a drunk; he was haunted. This sketch, his ramblings, he wasn't writing about *you*, was he?"

Pamela stared at the floor, suddenly unsteady.

"No," she whispered.

"Then who?" Myrna pressed gently.

"Who was the queen of the hive?" Pamela looked up. Her eyes were glistening.

"She was visiting just for the summer, a family cottage, I think. I don't know her first name, but everyone called her 'H'. Her last name started with a 'C,' Caplan, Copland...I'm not sure; it was a long time ago.

The name landed like a thunderclap. Dessa stiffened. Myrna's mouth parted, not in surprise, but in recognition. Her instincts had been right.

"H.C.," Pamela added.

"That's what she went by. I remember because it sounded lyrical, strange, but beautiful." Dessa said nothing. Myrna's hand hovered for a moment before resting lightly on Pamela's arm.

"Was she the one Crescent kept drawing?"

Pamela nodded slowly.

"He adored her, beautiful Black girl. Followed her around like a shadow. But something happened to her. Something awful. She left that summer and never came back." Dessa's voice was cold when she finally spoke.

"Did you know what they did to her?" Pamela's eyes went wide.

"Not at the time, but I pieced it together later."

"Did you help her?" Dessa asked.

"I was sixteen, and I was scared. And I didn't help her."

40

The Origin of the Kiss

At night, the world settled into a hushed stillness. Stars spilled across the sky in a glittering river, while fireflies blinked like tiny lanterns in the grass. The faint glow of porch lights shimmered along the shoreline, their reflections trembling on the dark water. From a distant cottage came bursts of laughter, carried easily across the lake, mingling with the soft strum of a guitar. The air was cool and smelled faintly of pine and smoke from a dying campfire. It was the kind of place where whispers seemed to vanish into the trees, where secrets could be kept, or buried, beneath the glassy surface of the lake, waiting to rise again like ghosts.

In July 1985, a fifteen-year-old girl stood just outside the screen door, barefoot on the warped wooden deck, holding a bottle of orange pop she hadn't asked for. She sat waiting for her new friend. About half an hour passed before, through the trees, she saw a single flashing light in the night; it was Pamela coming to meet her, dressed in acid-wash jeans and a Members-Only Jacket.

The hem of her floral sundress fluttered in the lake breeze. The woods crackled with insects and distant loons, and the warm air carried a hint of pine and charcoal from the evening bonfire the others had built down by the dock. She quickly put on her high-top sneakers before Pamela got to the steps. As they walked along, she could hear the laughter getting closer. The clinking of beer bottles, a splash, someone shouting dares over reggae music playing off a cheap boom box.

Pamela held the flashlight low, casting their shadows tall and jagged along the trees.

"Hey, Larry will be there tonight, said he'd save you a dance." H.C. tugged at the end of her floral dress.

"Larry, is he the one who keeps following me around?" Pamela smiled,

"He's kinda sweet." H. C. rolled her eyes,

"Gag me with a spoon." They both laughed.

"You sure this is the shortcut?"

"Relax," Pamela said, glancing back with a grin.

"We used to sneak through here all the time when we were kids."

"I just don't want to trip on a raccoon or something." Pamela laughed softly.

"You'd hear them first; they sound like angry toddlers." She paused, shining the light ahead,

"Anyway, it's not like I'd let anything happen to you."

"So, who's all there?"

"Everyone, Charles, Harry, Elias, Melissa... don't roll your eyes, I already know. Melissa's probably dancing on a picnic table by now." H. C. looked down at her shoes.

"How am I gonna avoid Larry Crescent?" Pamela slowly raised and lowered her shoulders.

"Don't know, he's been looking forward to seeing yuh all day."

H. C. groaned.

"Ugh, he's so weird. He barely talks, but he keeps staring at me like I'm gonna float away."

"Well," Pamela said, teasing,

"You do kind of have that moon-girl energy."

"I wish he'd like someone else. It's like… he doesn't know how to like someone properly. It's like he's… watching, always." Pamela's smile faltered for half a second.

"Yeah, Larry's always been off, but he's harmless. Just tell him you're not interested."

"I did, he just said, *you'll see.* Like it was some prophecy or something."

They fell into silence for a few paces, the flashlight's circle bobbing between roots and shadows. Then Pamela said quietly,

"You can hang with me tonight, stick close." H. C. glanced at her,

"Thanks." Pamela nodded, then suddenly said,

"Hey, Cohen…"

"What?" Pamela hesitated, the beam of the flashlight catching her own worried eyes in its spill.

"If you ever get that weird feeling around someone, like you're not safe, don't ignore it." H.C. wrinkled her forehead.

"Why are you saying that?" Pamela smiled again, but it didn't quite reach her eyes.

"Just girl talk, come on, almost there." And the trees opened ahead, spilling faint laughter and the flicker of bonfire light

"Come on, Cohen!" a voice called. It was Charles. His dreadlocks bounced when he moved into the frame, a crooked smile on his face.

"Why are you acting shy now? Thought you said you liked music."

"I do," she answered, cautiously stepping inside. The air was thick with weed, smoke and the sour stench of beer.

The living room had been rearranged, the couch pushed back, the table cleared, and blankets thrown over the floor. Someone had spilled chips in the corner. Elias Vogney stood near the speakers, shirtless, fiddling with the dial. Johnson was in the kitchen, pouring shots. Crescent was pacing, already buzzed, muttering to himself.

"H. C.!" Libra grinned again.

"You said you wanted to be one of us." She didn't remember saying that; maybe she had, but not like this. Something shifted then. The music lowered. The laughter quieted. She looked around, but no Pamela.

"Truth or dare," said Johnson, his voice hard with amusement.

"I'm good," she said, trying to back away.

"No, no, stay. Just one round." Libra touched her shoulder. She froze.

"Dare," said Vogney.

"We already know the truth's boring." She held the bottle tighter. Her hand trembled.

"Take off your shirt," Crescent said quietly, almost unsure. Then, louder, he added,

"We all want to see." Then Libra laughed.

"She's just waiting to be kissed." Michelle came into the room.,

"Hey, H, where's Pamela?" She turned to the door. Charles blocked it now.

"Leave her alone," Michelle said as she pushed past Libra.

She followed H.C.

The two girls looked around for Pamela, who had been sitting down by the docks. She had been sitting on the dock's edge alone, her knees pulled up to her chest, cigarette glowing between her fingers. The firelight behind her flickered across the lake's surface, warping her reflection into something ghostlike.

"Pamela!" Michelle called.

"You coming back in or what?" Pamela turned her head slightly but didn't stand.

"What's going on?"

"Something's off in there," Michelle said, her voice tense.

"Crescent's being a creep again, and Libra's acting like he owns the place. H.C. looks uncomfortable." Pamela noticed H.C. standing a few feet away, exhaled slowly, then took one last drag and tossed the cigarette onto the dock.

"Shit." She stood and wiped her hands on the back of her jeans, her jaw clenched. She walked past Michelle without a word, back toward the cabin.

Inside, the mood had darkened. Crescent muttered with his journal open on the arm of the couch, pages fluttering under the ceiling fan. Elias was pouring something sticky into a red Solo cup, and Johnson was laughing low under his breath. H. C. followed, stood in the middle of the room, back straight. Vogney clutched a bottle tight to his chest. He was frozen, caught between fear and confusion, unsure whether to run or pretend everything was fine.

Libra had just taken a step closer when Pamela's voice cracked through the air.

"Yo, back off."

The music stopped, and Crescent's muttering ceased. Johnson turned, surprise etched across his face. Pamela stepped fully into the room.

"She's going home." Libra raised an eyebrow.

"We're just playing."

"She's not playing," Pamela said.

"She's fifteen."

"So?" Johnson grinned.

"She came here, didn't she?"

"She came because I asked her to, not for this."

"I'll take you back," Pamela said, gently reaching for her arm.

"Let's go," but Crescent moved first, slamming his journal shut.

"She wanted to be Queen of the Hive," He slurred, words bleeding into one another.

"She said so; she was smiling all night."

"Don't listen to him," Pamela said to H. C.

"He doesn't know what he's saying."

"Larry, shut the fuck up!" Pamela's voice snapped like a whip.

"You don't know what you're saying." Michelle reappeared in the hallway, jaw set.

"You heard her." Silence.

Then Crescent backed into the wall, eyes wide and blinking. Johnson stared at Pamela, but said nothing. Elias poured himself another shot and looked away. Pamela led H. C. back out into the night, her hand firm but trembling. Behind them, the glittering lake mirrored the silence. The screen door creaked shut. And in that moment, the summer of 1985 fractured, remembered differently by everyone, but never truly forgotten by anyone. Not even by the one who survived. It was the origin of the kiss, not the kind given, but the type taken. A mark that echoed forward in silence, in shame, in blood.

41

The Wrappers She Kept

It began there with the first kiss, the last breath of innocence, and the birth of something colder. That morning, H.C. stayed mostly in bed, pretending to sleep, though her eyes had remained open long after the sunlight painted lines across the wooden floorboards. She'd heard Pamela's voice once or twice, muffled, apologetic, before Pamela left with Michelle to run into town for supplies.

Now it was evening again, Tuesday, July 9th. The lake was gold-tipped from the sunset, but everything else felt dull. The buzz of the previous night's party had been replaced with something quieter, more calculated. There was no music playing this time, just the sound of a screen door banging shut across the cove, and the occasional hiss of a lighter. She hadn't seen Pamela since noon. Michelle had promised to come back around dinnertime, but she hadn't. The older cousin who was supposed to be watching her left her alone with a bored apology and a pack of Lipton iced tea. The cottage felt empty, but not safe.

Around 8:00, there was a knock on the sliding door. It wasn't loud, just three slow taps. H.C. peeked through the curtain and saw Charles Libra on the porch, wearing a muscle tank, his dreadlocks pulled back, sunglasses still on though the sun had already dipped behind the trees.

"Pamela asked me to come get you," he said through the screen.

"She's down at the dock." H.C. hesitated. Something in her gut clenched.

"She asked for me?" she said faintly. Libra smiled.

"Said she was waiting."

She stepped out, barefoot again, not bothering with her shoes this time. The wood was warm under her feet. A few moths danced around the porch light, and the sky was thick with stars again.

"Is she mad at me?" H.C. asked as they walked down the path. Libra chuckled low.

"Nah. She didn't want you to be alone." But when they reached the dock, it was empty.

"She must've gone back inside," Libra said, scanning the shadows.

"She's not here," H.C. whispered, turning.

"Maybe I should go."

But then Elias appeared at the treeline, holding a flashlight. Crescent stood behind him, swaying slightly, holding a paper bag with a bottle inside. Johnson was already down by the fire pit, poking at it with a branch. And Pamela was nowhere. Vogney mumbled something cruel, a line H.C. would spend the next twenty years trying not to remember. H.C.'s breath caught. Her feet stopped moving.

"I think I'll just head back." Libra's hand came down gently but firmly on her shoulder.

"Relax, moon-girl. It's just a chill night. Truth or dare again. No pressure."

Crescent lifted the paper bag and grinned.

"We saved you a drink." H.C.'s eyes scanned the tree line again, hoping for a flashlight, for a voice, for Pamela. But the trees were still. And the stars above blinked down coldly, like they knew what was coming. Her voice barely came.

"Let me go!" Johnson chuckled and grabbed a chocolate kiss from his pocket, unwrapping it slowly.

"Don't be a buzzkill, H." The next few moments would never return in order; they fractured, broke apart, and reassembled only in shadows.

Four young men surrounded her. She screamed, and they dragged her into the cottage. The first chocolate kiss fell from Libra's hand and landed beside her cheek, still wrapped in silver foil. She stared at it, dazed. Even as they laughed, she hoped that Pamela would help her. Pamela would come, but she never did.

Hands. Voices. Shattering glass. Something sharp pressed into her back. The metallic crinkle of foil. The pain. As she was dragged, as she fought, they said you wanted to be part of the pact. She tried to turn and then, at the edge of her vision, Pamela, standing still, watching. Their eyes locked, both screaming without sound. But Pamela didn't move... not because she didn't want to, but because something had already broken inside her. They took turns; she memorized every moment.

When it was over, they threw a handful of kisses at her. One landed in her hair, then bounced to the ground.

"Now you're part of the hive," Libra said.

"Didn't Pamela tell you?" That night, she walked barefoot through the woods, pine needles sticking to her feet. Foil cutting her palms as she bled and clutched the candy wrappers in her fist. She screamed with rage, and her breath ragged like she was running from the whole forest. She would never tell her family.

Instead, she folded the wrappers into a box. A small pink box she carried through name changes and relocation, through silence and survival, the only proof she carried of the hive that tried to consume her.

42

Echoes of Kisses

Myrna returned to her desk and finally did what she'd been avoiding: she opened her evidence files and cross-referenced access logs. One person had been at every site. Every time something new turned up. Her fingers trembled as she circled a name. She stared at it, heart pounding. The division was unnervingly quiet.

A cup of tea gone cold beside her, the last of the January daylight bleeding into a murky dusk outside. She rubbed her temples, still aching from the confrontation earlier that afternoon. Sue's timeline hadn't matched the one Pamela had given them, and Britney's statement about the Honeycomb Pact kept echoing like a nursery rhyme twisted into something darker.

And now, standing at the edge of the woods, Myrna realized the forest didn't end. She turned to the stack of evidence logs and pulled the files toward her. Names. Dates. Scene reports. Sign-ins. Visitor records.

One by one, she went through them again, this time not looking for a clue, but for a presence, someone who was always just there. Not always obvious, sometimes in the margins. Sometimes explaining something away, sometimes even helping.

She flipped open a spiral-bound logbook. Her finger paused on an entry. A detail that had seemed harmless last week now hummed with quiet implication. Then another, and another. Myrna sat back, heart heavy. No name stood out, not yet, but the pattern was unmistakable.

Whoever it was hadn't needed to sneak in; they'd been welcomed, trusted, maybe even protected. She looked at the notes from the High School of Commerce teacher's logs, trying to fit the last pieces together. Each scribbled line, carrying echoes of kisses, silent markers left behind by someone who knew exactly where to hide.

The names blurred until one rhythm emerged, like a drumbeat hidden under noise. Michelle Campbell of Bells Corners. Married now, but still connected to the cheerleader pact. Myrna circled it hard enough to tear the page. She reached into her drawer and pulled out a photo, the one of the sketch labelled *Queen of the Hive*. Myrna studied the girl's eyes.

"Time to meet Michelle," she said under her breath.

Outside, snow began to fall, slow and unhurried. The address was scrawled on a sticky note in Myrna's pocket: Michelle Richards, formerly Michelle Campbell. A name that hadn't meant anything to her three days ago. Now it hummed with quiet weight. It had taken digging through Crescent's ramblings and re-reading Sue's vague recollections to connect the dots.

Michelle, cheerleader, cottage, and one of the few girls besides Pamela and Britney who might've known everything. The townhouse complex sat on Mill Hill Crescent, rows of modest, brick-faced homes stacked with wreaths and melting snowmen. It was quiet, the kind of quiet that felt earned. Myrna parked at the end of the lot, tucked her badge in her coat, and decided, for now, not to knock with authority.

She knocked like a neighbour instead. A child's voice shouted something inside. A dog barked once, then silence. The door creaked open, and there stood a woman with a braided ponytail and tired eyes, late thirties, maybe. Faint eyeliner smudged on her honey brown skin from the day. She wore a cardigan and jeans, and her smile was the kind that strangers offered when they expected to be asked for donations.

"Yes, can I help you?"

"Michelle Richards?" Myrna asked.

"That's me," the woman replied, cautious now. Myrna offered her hand.

"Detective Myrna Watkis. I was hoping you had a moment to talk about someone you knew a long time ago, Pamela Darah." The woman froze; her hand remained by her side.

"What is this about?"

"I promise I'm not here to make trouble. I'm looking into events from the summer of 1985."

"You were at a cottage then. You knew Pamela, Britney, possibly someone named H. C.?" Michelle hesitated. The name clearly struck her, though she recovered quickly.

"I remember the summer," she said.

"But that was twenty years ago."

"I know," Myrna said gently.

"But what happened that summer is still affecting people. Pamela's involved in something serious. Anything you remember, anything at all, could help."

Michelle exhaled slowly, then turned and looked down the

hallway.

"My kids are upstairs, give me a second."

She disappeared into the house. Myrna heard her speaking in a hushed voice, followed by the low hum of a television coming on. A moment later, Michelle returned, stepping out onto the porch, arms crossed against the cold.

"You can ask," she said, "But I'm not promising I can help." Myrna nodded.

"You knew about the Honeycomb Pact." Michelle flinched. Not visibly, but enough that Myrna caught it.

"That was just high school stuff."

"Pamela was assaulted that summer," Myrna said softly.

"And so was someone else, a girl with the initials H. C., she was fifteen. Were you there the night it happened?"

Michelle looked away, blinking hard.

"No, I wasn't at the cabin when it happened, but I saw Pamela the next morning. Her lip was bleeding, she said she'd fallen."

"And you believed her?" Michelle shook her head.

"I didn't want to believe anything else." Myrna took a breath. "What about the girl, H. C.?"

Michelle's voice dropped,

"She was sweet, quiet, and Pamela liked her a lot. Protected her, even. But something changed after that night. I remember... Pamela stopped looking anyone in the eye. And that girl, she left, just disappeared. No goodbyes, just gone."

"You kept the secret."

"We all did," Michelle said.

"Pamela begged us not to talk, said she had it handled, that the guys would leave her alone. That we didn't understand." Her voice faltered.

"We didn't. We were kids, too."

Myrna nodded.

"But now it's come back." Michelle looked down.

"It never really left." They stood in silence for a moment, breath fogging in the cold air.

"I have one more question," Myrna said.

"Did you see Pamela that second night? After the girl left?"

"No. I think... I think she was gone, too. Out in the woods somewhere. When she came back, she looked like she'd aged ten years."

Myrna's heart thudded.

"Did she ever say what happened?"

"No," Michelle said.

"But that was around the same time she started collecting them."

"Collecting what?" Michelle glanced back toward the house, toward her daughter's window.

"Dolls."

"Do you remember H.C.'s first or last name?" She paused, attempting to recall.

"Gosh, I wanna say yes, but it was so long ago. Maybe leave your card in case I remember."

Myrna thanked her and left. She wasn't sure of much about this case, but she was convinced now more than ever that Pamela was being set up.

Back in her car, Myrna sat behind the wheel, her fingers curled tightly around the steering wheel. The snow was coming down harder now, blanketing the windshield in a slow, steady sheet of white. Michelle's words echoed in her mind: She left, no goodbyes, just gone, like someone erased her.

A name still refused to surface, yet a face lingered in Myrna's mind, the sketch Crescent had drawn, labelled Queen of the

Hive, now more haunting than ever. Whoever that girl was, she had been there. She had seen everything. And now, after all these years, someone was either trying to defend her... or silence her for good.

Myrna flipped open her phone and dialled.

"Tech office," came the voice on the other end.

"Mark, it's Myrna. I need a favour."

"Sure thing, Detective. What've you got?"

"I'm sending over a scan of a sketch of a teenage girl, roughly fifteen, drawn by Crescent. Go ahead and run it through facial recognition databases. Missing persons, student records, hell, even archived ID photos if you can get them."

There was a pause.

"That important?"

Myrna stared through the windshield as the snow softened the world into silence.

"Yeah. She's the one this case is orbiting around, but I don't know who she is yet."

"Got it, send it now, I'll prioritize it."

She ended the call and pulled the sketch from the folder in her passenger seat, one more glance at those wide-set eyes and that haunted tilt of the jaw. Myrna took a photo and sent it.

As she sat in the stillness of the car,

"Let's find out what secrets you're still keeping, Queen of the Hive," she said, voice low, as if the sketch might answer back. Then she turned the key in the ignition and drove off. As she drove into the storm, she thought of the foil wrappers, the sketch, the pact. Every path circled back to the same face, the same kiss. Echoes that refused to die, no matter how deeply they'd been buried. A name still wouldn't come, but a face burned behind Myrna's eyes, the sketch Crescent had drawn, labelled Queen of the Hive, now more haunting than ever. She should have seen it sooner, the slope of the jaw, the sadness in those wide eyes. It wasn't just a drawing; it was a warning disguised as memory, a mirror she had refused to recognize. And now that face waited in silence, patient and unyielding, as though daring her to finally speak the name she had buried too deep, the one she could no longer ignore. Snow whispered against the windshield, a slow, relentless hush, and the city beyond blurred, as if refusing to release the face haunting her.

43

The Name Behind the Kiss

The office was still dark when Myrna arrived. The overhead fluorescents flickered awake one by one as if startled from sleep. She set her keys down with a dull clink, the echo swallowed by the hum of machines and the muffled whine of wind outside. The night hadn't given her much; just fragments of memory, Michelle's haunted eyes, and the growing certainty that something in this case had been rotting at its core for a long time.

She sipped lukewarm coffee and flipped through her notebook, still thumbing the sketch Crescent had drawn. That girl, her eyes, the sorrow behind them, had followed Myrna into sleep and back out again.

Her phone rang. She checked, and the number appeared to be Michelle's. She answered quickly.

"Hello?" A pause, then:

"I remembered her name." Myrna sat up straighter.

"The girl, H. C.?"

"Yes, I knew it would come back if I stopped trying so hard. It just hit me this morning. I was brushing my daughter's hair, and it hit me out of nowhere."

"What was it?"

"Hahdessa, Hahdessa Cohen." Myrna didn't respond right away. The name slid into her mind like a puzzle piece that had always belonged.

"I remember Pamela whispering it to her once," Michelle added, voice lower now.

"Like a secret she didn't want anyone else to hear."

Myrna scribbled it down, underlining it once.

"Thank you, Michelle." She hung up and stared at the name for a long time. Hahdessa Cohen. It sounded like something just under the surface, a name that should've rung louder. Her phone buzzed again.

Mark this time.

"You alone?" he asked.

"I am."

"I need you to come down here, right now, just you. You need to see this for yourself." Roads were slushy, and winter was working overtime to make the city feel abandoned. Streetlights flickered in the haze, and snow fell steadily in thick, lazy flurries. Her mind looped the name like a prayer: Hahdessa Cohen, Hahdessa Cohen. It meant something; it had to. She just hadn't connected it to the present yet.

At the division, Mark was waiting in the tech room, standing beside a flickering monitor, arms crossed, jaw tight. He didn't greet her with his usual tired grin. He looked rattled, or worse, like he didn't want to be the one to say what needed to be said.

"You okay?" Myrna asked. He motioned her in and shut the door behind her.

"You said this sketch was from that Crescent guy?"

"Yeah."

"And that it was important. cause everything was circling this girl?" Myrna nodded.

"Well," he exhaled,

"You were right."

I ran the sketch through the regular photo recognition software and got nothing, but then I tried the software used for missing people over time. He tapped a key, and the screen came to life. The sketch, Queen of the Hive, was on the left. On the right: a digital age progression, matched with facial structure points, landmarks, and symmetry indicators. Below was a growing list of matches. Most were low percentages. One... wasn't.

"Facial recognition pulled a 98.7% match from law enforcement databases," Mark said.

"At first, I thought it was a fluke. Sketches don't always scan well, but this one was precise. Almost too precise. Like the artist knew every feature by memory."

Myrna stepped closer, and the heat climbed up her neck, sudden and sharp.

"Who is it?" Mark hesitated.

"There's a match in the system. She's in our records, and not just passing through." She narrowed her eyes.

"A criminal file?" He shook his head.

"Internal." That made her stomach drop. Myrna looked up, mouth open, and stared straight at Mark. She said nothing.

"You sure you want to see this?" Mark spoke gently, as if bracing her for what came next. Myrna nodded slowly.

"Show me." Mark typed in a final command. The screen shifted. The images aligned, sketch to scan, past to present. Myrna's breath hitched.

She turned, looking right at Mark. She blinked once, twice,

as if trying to reset what she was seeing.

"Keep this between us for now." Mark gave a tight nod, understanding without needing an explanation.

Myrna stared back at the screen. The photo was clear now, not just a sketch or an outline pulled from someone's memory. It was her, Detective Dessa Simms. Younger, yes, a different hairstyle and fuller cheeks, but unmistakably the same woman who had been leading press conferences and reviewing case files with them for months. Myrna's breath hastened as the truth settled over her like a cold sheet. They had been searching for a ghost, chasing shadows, when the name behind the kiss had been sitting beside her all along.

"Jesus Christ," the name broke from her lips before she could stop it.

The memory slammed back with sickening clarity, the very first night, Libra's apartment. Myrna saw it again: the living room reeking of stale smoke, shadows stretching long under the furniture.

It was Dessa who had spotted the razor beneath the low coffee table, half-hidden in the dust. She'd crouched without hesitation, picked it up barehanded, then dropped it into an evidence bag like she was doing her job. Myrna had frowned at the time, ready to bark, Gloves, rookie! But Dessa brushed it off.

"Relax, first mistake of the night," she'd said, with that quick, crooked grin that made the others laugh and move on.

At the lab, only one set of fingerprints had come back on the razor, hers. Everyone, herself included, had shrugged it away. Of course, it was Simms. She bagged the evidence before putting her gloves on. That was the story. Nobody questioned it.

But now? Myrna's breath shook as the pieces rearranged themselves into something unforgiving. The razor hadn't just been evidence. It was the razor that had shorn Libra's hair. And the only person tied to it was Dessa.

Mark's voice cut into her spiralling thoughts.

"Yuh see it now, nuh true? All dis time, we thinking is an accident. But if she know we onto her?" He shook his head, muttering low.

"Whole ting mash up, Myrna. Whole damn ting."

Mark shifted back in his chair, eyes still on the screen, his grip tightened around the edge of his desk.

"She was in our system from a juvenile visit in 1985, assault complaint, no arrest. Different name then. Hahdessa Cohen. She changed it legally in '94 when she got married, two years before joining the academy."

Myrna blinked.

"That's why there was no immediate match. She scrubbed her past clean."

"She didn't scrub it. Just buried it deep enough, no one thought to look." Mark glanced up at her.

"Until now."

Myrna paced the small tech room, one hand at her mouth.

"And the cottage, she was there that summer."

Mark nodded grimly.

"The year of the assault."

Myrna's heartbeat thudded so loudly, it drowned out the room.

Myrna spun around.

"We don't say anything, not yet. We verify, we stay quiet. I'll review every case file she has worked on in the last six months. You lock this down. No one else sees it, not even the sergeant."

Mark frowned, running a hand down his face.

"Yuh know if she find out we onto her, it done."

Her eyes met his.

"Then we'd better move fast. Quiet and fast."

He sighed. "Mi can't believe it, star. All this time she deh right inna di middle, playin' both sides."

A heavy silence settled between them as the weight of what they'd uncovered began to sink in.

"I need the original files," she said at last, voice low, clipped.

"Everything connected to the juvenile case. No gaps."

Mark hesitated.

"You think she remembers?"

Myrna's gaze snapped to him.

"She wasn't acting like someone who forgot."

She took a step back from the monitor, then another, as though distance could undo what she'd just seen. Her heart wasn't racing; it was thudding, slow and deep, like footsteps coming up behind her in the dark.

"Lock this down," she repeated.

"Firewall it. I don't care if you have to pull the damn plug. No one sees it but us."

Mark gave a tight nod and turned back to the keyboard.

Myrna reached for the door, then paused. Her hand hovered over the knob.

"She looked me in the eye," she said, mostly to herself.

"Every day. Sat across from me like we were on the same side. And those damn notes!"

She opened the door.

"And the whole time..." Her voice dropped to a whisper.

"She knew."

Then she walked out the door, shutting it behind her with a

soft click, and Mark was left staring at the face on the screen, still frozen in time, watching and waiting.

44

Final Kiss

The hallway felt longer than usual, as though something in it had warped. Myrna walked it anyway, steady on the outside, chaos just beneath her skin. Every footstep echoed, too loud and too slow. She passed the squad room without looking in. Passed desks, chatter, the clatter of keys and boots and paper. Everything sounded normal, ordinary, unaware. But in her head, the image was still there, Dessa's face, merged with that old sketch like a ghost stitching itself into the present.

She made it to her office, shut the door, and braced against it. For a moment, she let herself feel it: the tightness in her chest, the heat rising behind her eyes. Betrayal, confusion, and something worse, fear; not for herself, but for what came next. She crossed to her desk, opened the drawer, and pulled out the case file, the one Dessa had insisted was going cold. Myrna flipped it open.

"Let's see what you buried."

She spent the next few hours going through that file and many others until she finally decided to stop ignoring Dessa's calls.

The wind swept gently over the lookout, rustling the maples that lined the ridge above the city. Dusk clung to the horizon, casting the Ottawa skyline in soft amber and violet, as if the world itself was pausing to hold its breath. Myrna stood at the edge of the path, arms crossed tight against the evening chill, a folder tucked beneath one elbow.

She could see everything from here: the Parliament buildings glowing faintly in the distance, the river like a ribbon of mercury below and the city lights flickering on like fireflies. It had been Dessa's idea to meet here.

"One last view before the world changes," she'd said on the phone. Her voice had been calm, too calm.

Myrna hadn't responded right away. She'd just looked at the name on her call display, heart pumping, unsure if she could still trust what she heard, or what she wanted to believe. Now, standing there in the fading light, the folder in her arms heavier than any she'd ever held, Myrna tried to steady herself. Inside were photos, logs, transcripts, Crescent's final sketches, and Pamela's statement. The doll parts, the wrappers, all of it pointing to the same name.

She'd spent the last thirty-six hours confirming what she hadn't wanted to face, cross-referencing files, checking entry logs, surveillance timestamps, re-reading Crescent's diary until her eyes blurred. Even the *Queen of the Hive* sketch, young, fragile, sad-eyed, made sense now.

Dessa had been everywhere, quietly, strategically; a ghost moving through the cracks of their investigation. Myrna heard footsteps behind her. She turned, and Dessa emerged from the shadows, wearing her long black coat and a scarf loosely draped around her neck. Her hair was down, caught in the wind. There was no badge on her hip. No notebook in her hand.

Only something behind her eyes that looked like goodbye.

"You came," Dessa said softly.

"It's peaceful up here, feels like you're not carrying the whole damn city on your shoulders."

Myrna didn't answer right away. She studied her partner, her friend, with aching clarity. Dessa continued.

"You left me no choice." A pause, the silence between them was fuller than any argument could've been.

"I thought maybe," Dessa said,

"If I showed you this place... you'd understand."

"I do understand," Myrna finally spoke.

"I just wish I didn't."

Dessa looked down at the folder in Myrna's arms,

"So you know."

"I know enough." Myrna steps forward slowly, quietly, but firmly. She outlines the case again, but this time, she's not seeking a confession. She already knows. Dessa listens with tears in her eyes. She doesn't deny it.

She confesses:

"I did it," she said quietly, eyes trained on the horizon.

"For the girl I used to be, for girls like her, like me, like Pamela." Her voice dropped, barely audible.

"No one listened, not then, so I made them hear me." She whispered into the wind. The breeze picked up, fluttering the edge of the folder. Myrna held it tighter; her fingers ached.

"I never wanted to hurt you, Myrna; you were too smart. You always were."

"But you did." Myrna's voice cracked.

"You lied. You made me chase ghosts while you stood beside me. And what about what you did to Pamela? Pamela was a victim, too." Something flickered in Dessa's expression, something sharp.

"Victim?" she said.

"No, she went quiet, she let them keep their crown."

"I didn't lie about everything."

"No, just the part where you were a killer." Dessa closed her eyes briefly,

"They deserved it!"

"Dessa, you committed murder."

"They were monsters."

Myrna stepped closer.

"You had me," she said, voice shaking.

"You had *me*, Dessa. You didn't have to do this alone."

Dessa's lips trembled,

"You would've stopped me."

"Maybe I should have." Another long pause. From her coat pocket, Dessa withdrew a small, silver-wrapped chocolate kiss. She held it between her fingers, its foil glinting in the half-light.

"One last one," she said.

"After this, I'm done." Myrna reached slowly for her phone.

"Don't," Dessa said, calm again.

"I'm not running. Seems I was wrong about Pamela. Looks like something similar happened to her."

"Yes, she was a victim, too," Myrna confirmed.

Dessa's demeanour changed immediately,

"No, not the same, she kept quiet and let them get away with what they did. I spoke up, but no one believed a little black girl."

"I read the report, but not much was in it."

"It was two weeks before I could find the courage to go in. I went alone, and by then, most of the evidence had been destroyed."

"And, you never told your parents?" Dessa paused, taking in air as though trying to fight back tears. A look of shame came over her face.

"No," she said.

Her other hand reached into her coat, slowly, deliberately, and pulled out a chocolate kiss. Myrna's eyes widened.

"Dessa, don't do this." But Dessa only smiled, her brown eyes damp.

"You said it yourself. Everything I touched was already broken." A single tear tracked down Myrna's cheek.

"Please, I won't let you do this."

Before Myrna could move, Dessa slipped the foil open with steady hands and placed the chocolate on her tongue. For a second, her eyes met Myrna's, pleading, defiant, both at once. Her fingers trembled for the first time.

"I'm sorry," she hushed, then she swallowed. The silver wrapper fluttered from her fingers as her knees buckled. Myrna moved quickly to her side.

"Dessa!" she screamed, her voice breaking.

"Why didn't I see it sooner? Why?"

A strangled gasp escaped, then silence. She reached for the note in Dessa's hand. It read:

This little girl,
ruined by her first kiss
Innocence lost and ever missed
Ever embedded in darkness,
I sought to find my justice.
The idea of prison makes me frown,

> *I'm not cut out to be locked down.*
> *So I won't be going there,*
> *Since it's something I could never bear.*
> *Goodbye partner.*
> *P.S. "Tell Bartlett I'm sorry... I wanted to say yes."*
> *Dessa.*

Myrna is stunned, staring at the lifeless form beside her. She realizes that Dessa might have chosen life if she'd believed she deserved it. She should have cuffed her. She should have said the words sooner. But all Myrna could do now was kneel in the cold, clutching the last note of a woman who had been her partner, her friend, and her ghost.

Myrna stood on the ridge, the wind pressing against her coat. The city lights blinked below like indifferent stars. She lifted her phone with numb fingers and forced the words out:

"Officer down."

45

Aftertaste

The scent of chocolate still hung faintly in the air, bittersweet and wrong. It clung to the room like a memory, one that wouldn't scrub clean no matter how hard anyone tried. Myrna stood over the body, unmoving. Her eyes traced the still hand curled near the note, the foil wrapper from the final kiss glinting like a shard of guilt in the low light.

Outside, blue and red lights spun silently against the night, painting the walls in alternating waves of justice and failure. Someone behind her called out,

"Time of death called at 12:17."

The wind carried the words away almost before they landed. Snow dusted across the ridge, catching in Myrna's hair, softening the hard lines of the moment. Red and blue lights bled into the trees, throwing long, broken shadows across the ground. The foil wrapper glinted where it had fallen, half-buried already by drifting flakes, a shard of silver against the dark earth.

Myrna didn't move. Around her, the scene unfolded with its own quiet rhythm: paramedics stepping back, officers speaking in low tones, evidence markers pressed into the frozen soil. The ridge seemed to absorb their voices, as if the earth itself refused to echo them.

Mark stood a few feet away, arms folded tight against the cold, his eyes fixed. When her gaze lifted to his, no words passed. He just nodded once, the smallest acknowledgment between people who understood too much.

Snow clung to Dessa's scarf, to her lashes, to the final note still crumpled in her hand. Myrna wanted to take it back before the bag swallowed it, before the chain of custody made it sterile. But she only stood there, the ache settling deeper into her bones, while the wind whispered through the maples like a chorus that would not end.

Myrna didn't respond. Her gaze stayed locked on another piece of the paper found inside Dessa's pocket. The words were scribbled in a trembling hand, unlike the first note they'd found all those months ago.

To Bartlett:

I'm sorry, love, I let it fall,
A yes unspoken, lost to all.
Sweet as spring rain, soft and true,
But never given, never you. If I could turn time anew, I'd give that,
yes, my heart to you. I'm sorry, Bartlett, that I fell—
The kiss you'd give, I could not tell.
The yes you held, sweet as spring rain,
I let it fall and bear the pain.
You sought to ask; I could not stay,
So took the last kiss and slipped away,
Dessa

A shallow ache settled in Myrna's chest, heavy and persistent. The woman who had outsmarted them all, who had stalked shadows for retribution, lay still, no longer a threat, no longer anyone.

"What now?" Mark's voice cracked behind her.

Myrna turned slowly. Her mouth opened, then closed again. What was now? A case closed, maybe. But nothing felt resolved, not really. The story had ended, yes, but it left behind a bitter aftertaste, something you couldn't spit out or swallow.

She looked back at the body.

"She wanted to be heard," Myrna said quietly.

"That's all she ever wanted."

Mark nodded, eyes glassy.

"She did."

And then, almost as an afterthought, Myrna added,

"She was also right about most of them, about what they did."

The silence that followed was thick. It was hard to breathe through. Injustice had started it. Love had twisted it. And revenge had finished the job. But somewhere in the middle of all that, a girl no one had saved tried to save herself.

A few days later, Myrna met Grant at the same hilltop. The air was clearer up there, away from the city's noise and the weight of the station. Myrna stood on the same hill where they'd once joked about retirement and bad knees, where Bartlett had shared his wild theories and somehow made them sound poetic.

She heard Grant's footsteps behind her, but didn't turn. He stood beside her for a while, saying nothing, just watching the trees sway below. The sky was the same soft gray as it had been the day the case broke open, the kind of sky that made everything feel like a memory.

She struggled to talk about it, the betrayal, the grief, the friendship. She stared at him, blinking in the wind.

"I don't know how to talk about it," Myrna said finally.

"The case... her, what she did, what we missed."

"She fooled everyone," Grant said quietly.

"But not out of cruelty. I think she just wanted... to feel powerful again."

Myrna nodded. Her throat was tight.

"And somewhere in all that madness, she loved him."

"Grant pulled a small velvet box from his pocket, flipping it open. Inside, the ring glimmered in the dying light. Grant said softly,

"He was going to propose. Two weeks ago, he told me." Wanted to wait until the case was over. I thought you should know,"

Myrna's body trembled a little. Something twisted deep in her gut, not just grief, but guilt.

"It's beautiful, he never said a word."

"He wanted to make sure she was the one first. Said he had a feeling, and when the case closed, he'd ask." Myrna closed her eyes; there was nothing to say. She turned away, the tears came quietly, not dramatic, not loud; just a leaking ache that wouldn't stay buried. Grant held her close.

"She wrote in the note," she said, voice hoarse.

"That she was going to say yes." Grant nodded, rubbing her back.

"Maybe that was the one honest thing she ever wrote."

The studio was quiet except for the steady hiss of rain against the windows. Pamela sat before a blank canvas, brush in hand, the smell of turpentine heavy in the air. The news had already spread: Detective Dessa Simms, the woman the papers now whispered was the killer, was dead.

Pamela couldn't bring herself to feel relief. Instead, a hollow weight pressed against her ribs, making it hard to breathe. She had lived under suspicion for months, her name dragged through the mud, every painting she touched judged as evidence of guilt. She should be furious, and part of her was, but the anger tangled itself with something more complicated, something darker.

If she had spoken years ago, if she had told the truth when the truth might have mattered, maybe the men would be in prison. Maybe Dessa would still be alive. Perhaps none of this would have ever happened.

Her hand trembled as she dipped the brush into black paint. The first stroke slashed the canvas, harsh and jagged. Another followed, crimson layered over the black, a raw wound spreading wide. Anger poured out of her in thick, unsteady lines. But then, almost without thinking, her strokes softened. Blue bled into the canvas, pale pink brushed against the edges, as though her grief was seeping in to dilute the rage. Her phone buzzed on the worktable, unknown number, then voicemail. She didn't press play. Instead, she lifted a smaller brush and worked a thin line of gold along the figure's shoulder, not a halo, not mercy, just the suggestion of light finding a path through cloud.

On the taboret, a neat row of foil squares lay flattened beneath a jar—wrappers she'd kept without admitting why. She slid one into the wet paint, pressed, lifted. A faint honeycomb impressed itself across the lower corner of the canvas, barely visible unless you knew to search.

Pamela stared at the mark until her throat hurt. Then she

wrote a title on the masking tape at the stretcher's edge: Aftertaste.

Only then did she listen to the voicemail. Sue's voice, thin and breathless:

"I'm sorry for all of it. If you ever want to... talk." Her voice cracked at the end, then silence. The message ended with the sound of someone deciding not to cry.

Pamela set the phone down. The rain pressed harder against the glass. The figure on the canvas did not move, but somehow it felt less alone.

By the time she stepped back, the canvas was no longer blank but haunted: a shadow of a girl dissolving into rain, one hand lifted as though reaching for something just beyond her grasp. The figure was neither villain nor victim, but both, fragile, broken, defiant.

Pamela set the brush down and pressed a paint-streaked hand against her chest, feeling her heart race. The painting wasn't finished, but maybe that was the point. Some wounds didn't resolve. Some stories didn't close neatly.

She whispered to the empty room,

"I hope you found your peace, Dessa. Because all I taste now is the aftertaste." For the first time in weeks, Pamela felt the weight shift, not gone, but lighter. The painting stared back at her, both a confession and an absolution. Two weeks later, Myrna stood at the edge of the lake where the trees still held the shape of old summers. The dock boards were rimed with frost; her breath hung and then vanished. She didn't bring evidence. She brought nothing at all.

Across the water, a cottage light blinked once and went dark. Somewhere, a loon called out of season like a mistake the world hadn't corrected. Myrna crouched and traced a small hexagon in the thin ice along the shore, then another, until a crooked honeycomb spidered out from her glove.

"We remembered," she said, not loud, not soft, just enough for the cold to carry it.

The ice skin cracked and healed itself in a shimmer. She straightened, pockets empty. The case in her mind closed along a seam that would never quite lie flat. As she turned back up the path, the lake kept its own counsel, as lakes do. But the air felt cleaner. Or maybe she did.

Now there was only silence. Grant and Myrna stood holding each other in the hush of wind and dusk, the hills stretching endlessly ahead of them. Below, the city continued to move, unaware of what had almost happened. And just like that, sweetness curdled. Only silence, and a name no one would forget, Hahdessa Cohen, the name behind the kiss.

Also by Daidra Senior

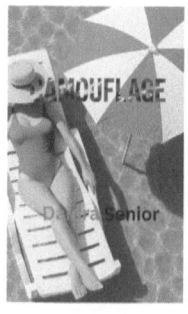

Camouflage
In this gripping mystery novel, Courtney finds herself entangled in a web of secrets following the shocking death of someone close to her. As she struggles to understand the distance between herself and her mother, she's haunted by the possibility that Derrianne, someone she once trusted, might be capable of murder.

But the mystery deepens. A strange woman keeps appearing, a cryptic chest holds untold secrets, and Courtney must piece together a puzzle that threatens to unravel everything she thought she knew. With suspense, emotional tension, and unexpected twists, Camouflage explores the hidden truths that lie beneath the surface of family, identity, and trust.

Thank you for reading *Kisses from a Killer*.

This novel is the beginning of a gripping series, and the story is just getting started.

To keep track of new releases, updates, and exclusive content from the series, visit:

www.daidrasenior.substack.com

www.ingramcontent.com/pod-product-compliance
Lightning Source LLC
Chambersburg PA
CBHW020358080526
44584CB00014B/1077